Since 20 December 2001 – the date which marked the authorization of the International Security Assistance Force (ISAF) to assist the Afghan Government – hundreds of thousands of coalition soldiers from around 50 different states have physically been and served in Afghanistan. Roughly 20 rotation periods have been experienced; billions of US dollars have been spent; and almost 3,500 coalition soldiers and 7,400 Afghani security personnel have fallen for Afghanistan. In this badly-managed success story, the true determiner of both tactical outcomes on the ground and strategic results was always the tribal and rural parts of Muslim-populated Afghanistan.

Although there has emerged a vast literature on counterinsurgency theories and tactics, we still lack reliable information about the motivations and aspirations of the residents of Tribalized Rural Muslim Environments (TRMEs) that make up most of Afghanistan. The aim of this book is to describe some on-the-ground problems of counterinsurgency (COIN) efforts in TRMEs – specifically in rural Afghanistan – and then to propose how these efforts might be improved. Along the way, it will be necessary to challenge many current assumptions about the conduct of counterinsurgency in Afghanistan. Generally, this book will show how counterinsurgency succeeds or fails at the local level (at the level of tactical decisions by small-unit leaders) and that these decisions cannot be successful without understanding the culture and perspective of those who live in TRMEs.

Although engaging issues of culture, the author is not an anthropologist or an academic of any kind. He is a Muslim who spent his childhood in a TRME – a remote village in Turkey – and he offers his observations on the basis of 15 years' worth of field experience as a Turkish Special Forces officer serving in rural Iraq, Turkey, Kazakhstan, Kyrgyzstan and Afghanistan. Cultures in these areas are not the same, but there are sufficient similarities to suggest some overall characteristics of TRMEs and some general problems of COIN efforts in these environments.

In summary, this book not only challenges some of the fundamentals of traditional counterinsurgency wisdom and emphasizes the importance of the tactical level – a rarely-studied field from the COIN perspective – but also blends the first-hand field experiences of the author with deep analyses. In this sense, it is not solely an autobiography, but something much more.

After graduating from the Turkish War Academy in 1998, Metin Gurcan joined the Turkish Special Forces and served in Afghanistan, Kazakhstan, Kyrgyzstan, Kosovo and Iraq as a military adviser/liaison officer from 2000-2008.

In 2008-2010, he got his MA degree in Security Studies from the US Naval Postgraduate School, Monterey. In 2010-2014, he worked as an analyst officer in the Turkish General Staff.

In 2014, Gurcan worked as a visiting research fellow at Changing Character of War (CCW), Oxford University, on counterinsurgency efforts in tribal and Muslim settings. After resigning from the military, Gurcan got his PhD at Bilkent University/Ankara in April 2016 with a dissertation which was titled 'Opening the Blackbox: The Transformation of the Turkish Military'. Gurcan has another forthcoming book about the Gallipoli Campaign to be published in August 2016. He has been published extensively in Turkish and foreign academic journals about the changing nature of warfare, terrorism, Turkish civil-military relations, military history and Turkish foreign policy.

What Went Wrong in Afghanistan

Understanding Counterinsurgency Efforts in Tribalized Rural and Muslim Environments

Metin Gurcan

 Helion & Company Limited

Helion & Company Limited
26 Willow Road
Solihull
West Midlands
B91 1UE
England
Tel. 0121 705 3393
Fax 0121 711 4075
Email: info@helion.co.uk
Website: www.helion.co.uk
Twitter: @helionbooks
Visit our blog http://blog.helion.co.uk/

Published by Helion & Company 2016
Designed and typeset by Mach 3 Solutions Ltd (www.mach3solutions.co.uk)
Cover designed by Paul Hewitt, Battlefield Design (www.battlefield-design.co.uk)
Printed by Lightning Source Limited, Milton Keynes, Buckinghamshire

Text © Metin Gurcan 2016
Illustrations © Metin Gurcan 2016
Maps © as individually credited

Cover: Public domain image

ISBN 978-1-911096-00-9

British Library Cataloguing-in-Publication Data.
A catalogue record for this book is available from the British Library.

All rights reserved. No part of this publication may be reproduced, stored in a retrieval system, or transmitted, in any form, or by any means, electronic, mechanical, photocopying, recording or otherwise, without the express written consent of Helion & Company Limited.

For details of other military history titles published by Helion & Company Limited contact the above address, or visit our website: http://www.helion.co.uk

We always welcome receiving book proposals from prospective authors.

To Senem…

Contents

List of Illustrations	viii
Foreword	ix
Preface	xi
1. What is Tribalized Rural Muslim Environment (TRME)?	29
2. Afghanistan: A View from the Ground	67
3. The Other Side of the COIN in Afghanistan	92
4. Conclusion	126
Bibliography	132
Index	135

List of Illustrations

Figures

1 The components of the Taliban-led insurgency. (Author's own illustration) 75
2 A chart portraying rural Afghanistan. 101

Maps

1 Topography of Afghanistan. 69
2 Ethnolinguistic groups in Afghanistan. 72
3 Taliban presence in Afghanistan as of 2015. 74

Foreword

When Metin Gurcan first came to visit me, he brought his laptop and showed a video to me and my three sons. On the screen several soldiers in camouflage uniforms were holding up a large paper target with a chest-sized black rectangle on it. Gurcan was standing with them, and talking with them. Then he paced away from the soldiers perhaps 10 meters' distance. He stopped, turned around to face the soldiers, raised his pistol and fired several rounds at the target they were holding. Then he turned again, facing away from the soldiers, bent down from the waist and fired several more rounds at the target, firing upside down between his legs. 'Trust fire' is what he called this ritual, a means of building trust among soldiers: trust in their skills, trust in one another.

I recall thinking that day that our visitor was an unusual person, living between action and scholarship. His research was also unusual. From his experience soldiering in Afghanistan he had come to a view of Western counterinsurgency operations that was unlike anything I had seen before.

Most analyses of Afghanistan portray three actors locked in conflict: the Taliban, a fundamentalist Islamic group that gave refuge to al-Qaeda; the US and NATO Coalition Forces fighting Taliban and al-Qaeda; and the warlords, such as Ismail Khan and Abdul Rashid Dostum, who joined with Coalition Forces against the Taliban.

The unhappy history of these three actors is complex[1] but can be briefly summarized. Warlords were empowered by the US and Pakistan to fight the Russians in Afghanistan; were suppressed by the Taliban after the Russians departed; were resurrected by the US to fight the Taliban after the 9/11 attacks; and are currently resisting centralization of power in Kabul even as they prepare to face the Taliban again when US Forces depart Afghanistan.

In this history, inhabitants of the tribalized, rural, Muslim environment of the conflict (Gurcan's TRME) are a passive and suffering background. Local people are exploited, threatened, and killed by the Taliban, by Coalition Forces, and by warlords.

---

1 Antonio Giustozzi, *Empires of Mud: Wars and Warlords in Afghanistan* (New York: Oxford University Press, 2009).

They seek security, and counterinsurgency doctrine says that victory will in the end go to whichever of the three strong actors can best provide physical security.

In this book, Gurcan offers a different view. The locals are not passive victims but active agents trying to survive and prosper in the conflicts they cannot avoid. Much of the violence in Afghanistan, and particularly the location and targeting of violence, is determined by local people trying to protect their income, their honor, and their pastures. As Gurcan makes clear, illiterate does not mean stupid. Local people learn how to advance their own interests in the interstices of conflict between giants. Often enough, in a land where honor depends on violence, local interests lead to violence.

Recognizing the agency of local people in a counterinsurgency problem is a conceptual advance. The locals are not just suffering violence while waiting for powerful others to provide security. Equally important, however, is Gurcan's recognition of the limited power of ideology for understanding when and where violence challenges counterinsurgency forces. In a TRME, Islam is neither the beginning nor the end of violence. Survival, justice, and honor are the motors of violent action by local people, not religion. This recognition parallels research showing the importance of local interests in the occurrence of violence in civil war.[2] Of course there are ideologies in competition in Afghanistan. The Taliban advance a fundamentalist one-size-fits-all version of Islam, and Coalition Forces advance a fundamentalist one-size-fits-all version of democratic state building. But warlords have no ideology but power, and local people are more concerned with family and tribal interests than any broader ideology. At the tactical level, Gurcan shows us that ideology has little to do with success or failure of counterinsurgency operations. This is an important lesson for Westerners whose newspapers too easily translate TRME violence into 'Muslim violence'.

I am pleased to say that the beginnings of this new book were first published as an article in *Dynamics of Asymmetric Conflict*[3] while I was editor of the journal. The title of that article is worth revisiting: 'Between heaven and earth: Field observations relating to counterinsurgency in tribalized rural Muslim environments'. The new book takes Gurcan's thinking a long way forward, especially with regard to lessons for soldiers engaged in counterinsurgency, as he continues to build from hard experience on earth toward higher and broader conceptions of that experience.

Clark McCauley
Research Professor of Psychology
Bryn Mawr College

2   Stathis N. Kalyvas, *The Logic of Violence in Civil War* (Cambridge: Cambridge University Press, 2006).
3   Metin Gurcan, 'Between heaven and earth: Field observations relating to counterinsurgency in tribalized rural Muslim environments', *Dynamics of Asymmetric Conflict: Pathways toward terrorism and genocide,* 2:2 (2009), pp.86-111.

Preface

> Human beings are members of a whole, in creation of one essence and soul.
> If one member is afflicted with pain, other members uneasy will remain.
> If you have no sympathy for human pain, the name of human you cannot retain.
>
> Sa'adi Shirazi, 13th century Islamic poet

Traditional wisdom[1] defines *insurgency* as an important part of unconventional war or a form of irregular conflict aiming to overthrow a constituted government through the use of subversion and armed conflict.[2] Stated another way, an insurgency is an organized, protracted politico-military struggle designed to weaken the control and legitimacy of an established government, occupying power, or other political authority while increasing insurgent control.[3] According to the US Government Counterinsurgency Guide (2009), counterinsurgency (COIN) may be defined as 'comprehensive civilian and military efforts taken to simultaneously defeat and contain insurgency and address its root causes'.[4]

For anyone seeking to understand to what extent these definitions fit into the realities on the ground in the contemporary global security environment, Afghanistan emerges as the first test case, as in the last decade we have witnessed a global mobilization to fight against the insurgency there. Since 2001, more than 500,000 coalition soldiers from 50 different countries have served in Afghanistan as part of the COIN operation. More than 16 rotation periods have been experienced and almost 800 billion USD spent, 3,400 coalition soldiers and around 8,000 Afghani security

---

1 This book is the developed version of Metin Gurcan's below-presented earlier publications: Metin Gurcan, 'Between heaven and earth: Field observations relating to counterinsurgency in tribalized rural Muslim environments', *Dynamics of Asymmetric Conflict*, 2: 2 (2011), pp.86-111. Metin Gurcan, 'Seeing the Other Side of the COIN: Problematization of 'Our' COIN efforts in Afghanistan' *Istanbul Policy Center (IPC) Report*, (February 2016).
2 *US Counterinsurgency Field Manual 3-24* (2006), p.1.
3 US Government Counterinsurgency Guide, *U.S. Government Interagency Counterinsurgency Initiative*, (January 2009), p.6.
4 Ibid.

personnel have fallen, roughly 100,000 civilians have lost their lives, and more than 50,000 soldiers have been injured so far.⁵ Are all these losses justified by what the international community has achieved in Afghanistan? This question, in fact, directly relates to the question of how one can define the overall outcome of our, the international Coalition Forces' (CF), Afghanistan experience. Is it an absolute victory, only a victory, a defeat, or even a total fiasco? Could it be, in the words of US President Barack Obama, a 'badly managed success story?'⁶

In my view, Afghanistan is indeed a success story at the tactical level in the sense that, at least as of today, the majority of Afghanis still hope for a more prosperous, democratic, and stable Afghanistan in the future. The high turnout rate of the 2014 presidential elections, despite the Taliban's attempts to disrupt the process, is proof of this argument. Further, nearly two-thirds of the voters in this election were under the age of 25. Simply speaking, Afghanistan has not fallen into total chaos at the moment. But we should admit that this success story was badly managed at the strategic-political level in the sense that things did not go as we assumed at the initial phase, and every actor involved shares responsibility for this mismanagement. In this sense, the Afghanistan experience reflects the paradox in the contemporary COIN theaters. That is, although Afghanistan is a total victory in the military sense at the tactical level, coalition countries could not translate this military victory into a success story at the strategic-political level. Indeed, in a presentation I attended in Oxford's Changing Character of War (CCW) Program, a British lieutenant colonel emphasized the fact that since 2001 the CF in Afghanistan engaged in around 220 tactical and operational (battalion and brigade level) campaigns and did not lose any one of them.⁷ Similarly, Ret Major Jim Gant, a US Special Forces Team commander who served in Iraq and Afghanistan several times, emphasizes the tactical success in Afghanistan, but with a fundamental question regarding the tactical/strategic paradox:

> The US has been in Afghanistan for more than a decade. We have fought hard and accomplished some good. Tactically, we have not lost a battle. We defeat the Taliban in every engagement. But are we closer to our goals than we were a decade ago?⁸

---

5 Amy Belasco, 'The Cost of Iraq, Afghanistan, and Other Global War on Terror Operations Since 9/11,' *CFR Report*, (8 December 2014) <http://www.fas.org/sgp/crs/natsec/RL33110.pdf> (accessed 26 December 2015).
6 'Obama flips on Afghanistan Withdrawal Plan', *Huffington Post*, (15 October 2015), <http://www.huffingtonpost.com/entry/obama-afghanistan-withdraw-droops_us_561f7bebe4b0c5a1ce6217e2>
7 Presentation by a British Lt Col who served in Afghanistan, Oxford University's Changing Character of War (CCW) Program (9 January 2015).
8 Jim Gant, *A Strategy for Success in Afghanistan: One tribe at a time*, (Nine Sisters Imports: Los Angeles, 2009). Full report by Major Jim Gant, accessed 17 August 2015: <http://www.globalsecurity.org/military/library/report/2009/2009_one_tribe_at_a_time.pdf> (accessed 11 January 2016).

This question may appear rudimentary at first; however, it is such questions that are often overlooked when analyzing such modern-day conflicts. This book will therefore present the 'whats' and 'whys' of such a tactical-strategic paradox in light of the war in Afghanistan. In its first part, this book addresses the necessity of taking into account the perspectives, expectations, and strategies of the local population, and delineates the importance of modern armies in adapting to local circumstances by seeking to elucidate the tactical level COIN dynamics through the eye of a Muslim officer who served in many COIN theaters in the globe.

As a soldier-scholar trying to understand the changing character of conflict in the 21st century, this widening and deepening disconnect between the strategic-political level and tactical level is in fact my observation from the field, which then turned into my academic area of interest. As a former member of the Turkish Armed Forces, I served in many volatile regions of the globe to fight against extremism and terrorism at the tactical level. My 12-year career in the Turkish Special Forces (SF) led me to serve in many Tribalized Rural Muslim Environments (TRMEs). In fact, the phenomenon of TRMEs is relevant to my early life since I was born and raised in a remote village in Central Anatolia, which is a sort of tribalized and rural Muslim environment. During my service, I participated in many joint operations and exercises, and then fulfilled liaison and training missions in the hostile regions of rural Iraq (1999, 2003, 2005), Kazakhstan (2004), Kyrgyzstan (2004), and Afghanistan (2005) against Salafi extremism. From these experiences, as well as academic research, I have come to conclude that without problematizing the paradox splitting the strategic and local level, and reflecting on the whats and whys of this paradox, it is impossible to derive lessons useful for tackling future challenges.

As you may notice at the end of the book, the COIN experience in Afghanistan explicitly underlined the distinction between 'planning' and 'design'. While both activities seek to formulate ways to bring about preferable futures, they are cognitively different. The overall argument of this book is that, at the initial phase, Coalition Forces were too busy to solve problems in Afghanistan with the traditional cognitive and material tools and thus could not find time to define the exact problem in Afghanistan and set the problems in the Afghani way. Afghanistan proved that in hybrid settings general planning is not enough to adapt to an unorthodox situation. This book then contends that, in hybrid settings like Afghanistan, modern security actors of the world need new designs, preferably asymmetric ones, which zoom closer into the nature of an unfamiliar conflict in order to conceive of a framework for problem solving.

In fact, the implications of this strategic confusion of the international community about the design of the war in Afghanistan led to ambiguities in the efforts of the Coalition Forces. Though there has emerged a sizable literature about the current dilemma of the CF in Afghanistan, one, for instance, cannot still find clear answers of these very basic questions. What were the strategic objectives of the CF in Afghanistan? Were they trying to 'win a war against extremists' or 'rebuild Afghanistan?' Or were they trying to fulfill these two objectives, the accommodation of which at the same time was highly unlikely in military terms, *simultaneously*? Or were they planning to apply a 'that is all we could do folks, bye bye' strategy and wash their hands from Afghanistan?

Why is the TRMEs an important phenomenon which should be addressed accurately by the international community? Let me share one of my observations at this point. In every rural territory I served, I saw that anybody who is lucky enough to find a generator and a satellite phone has been trying to open an internet café. I was told many times by the entrepreneurs of this thorny business that if there were not a demand and profit, nobody could bother himself to start. They have also added that roughly all of their customers are under the age of 20. The demographic facts in TRMEs confirm these internet café owners. In Afghanistan, 60 percent of the population is under the age of 25.[9] This is the case as well for other countries such as the ones in the Middle East and Central Asia. Wherever I went, I witnessed the same phenomenon of youth bulge and internet-mania in TRMEs.

Besides, it should be stressed that the definition of 'poverty' is highly relevant in this case. How do we define poverty? My definition is the existence of an economic motivation but the absence of the socio-economic power to undertake it. For instance, if you have never seen a mobile phone in your life, it does not mean that you are deprived of a mobile phone since you have no knowledge of their existence – thus no motivation. But if you aware the existence of the mobile phone and you feel that you need one, then you have poverty if you cannot afford it. You have full knowledge, full motivation, but unfortunately no economic power to purchase it. Increasing internet usage and easy access to media outlets in TRMEs have not only reshaped the worldviews of younger generations by reducing their sense of isolation, but also have increased their ambitions, and their awareness of important political phenomena such as their government's failings to wipe out prevalent poverty.

In the same vein, the youth bulge in TRMEs has been associated with drastic socio-economic problems such as illiteracy and unemployment – the estimates of unemployment in Afghanistan, for instance, range as high as 80 percent.[10] Given the phenomena of increasing internet usage and easy access to the media outlets in TRMEs, combined with the youth bulge, it is not exaggerated to assert that the Pandora's Box has opened for millions of TRME youth. I would suggest that the international community has a great responsibility to answer this knotty question: which political rhetoric would satisfy the residents of the TRMEs? If TRMEs are abandoned by the international community to the extremists, the consequence of this fatal mistake would be very dire globally. The result would be a protracted and grim 'chaos' in the international system.

---

9   Ahmed Rashid, *Jihad: the Rise of Militant Islam in Central Asia*, (New York: Penguin Books, 2002), p.11. Also: <https://www.cia.gov/library/publications/the-world-factbook/geos/af.html> (accessed 11 January 2016).
10 Shireen Hunter, "Religion, Politics and Security in CA" *SAIS Review* (Summer 2001), p.78.

Unfortunately, though alarms bells have been ringing, the signs of 'strategic exhaustion' have become visible in the international community on any issue concerning the TRMEs, and a sense of 'ignorance' – even insult – has dangerously been growing with every passing month in the Western world.

For some, for instance, Afghanistan is a backward and largely illiterate country where donkeys deliver ballot boxes, and where people are stuck in medieval times.[11] Britain's then defense minister, Liam Fox, insulted Afghanistan, for instance, by describing it as a 'broken 13th-century country'.[12] Erik Prince, former CEO of the Blackwater private military company, declared that the Taliban were 'barbarians' who 'crawled out of the sewer' with 'a 1200 A.D. mentality'.[13] These were remarks that identify 'the West' with advanced science and technology, and confer an intoxicating sense of 'superiority' on Westerners. This fallacy places less technological societies further back on the timeline of advancement, so that people may falsely conclude that TRMEs are stuck in a time several centuries ago. The power of metaphor of technological progress on a time line may blind us to the fact that the people currently endeavoring to live in TRMEs are still our 'contemporaries'. Even those owners of the donkey carrying ballot boxes, the people driving horse carts, the people living in sewer-like places are part of a contemporary world. Forcing ourselves to acknowledge this apparently simple fact may also help us become aware of the relevance of TRME problems in the modern world.

One should also note that Afghanistan in 1200 AD, or *Khorasan*, was a region of peace, tolerance and wisdom. Afghanistan was the soil which gave birth to Mawlana Rumi, Jami of Heart, Ansari, Sanayi of Ghazni and hundreds of more scholars, poets and philanthropists. Simply put, Afghanistan in 1200 AD was one of the stars of its era, the light of which enlightened the human history, and therefore was much more advanced from contemporary Afghanistan in terms of religious tolerance and peaceful coexistence. I would advise anybody challenging this argument to read one or two pages from the *Mathnawi*, a poetry book of Mawlana Rumi which was written in the late 1200s. Interestingly, I wish we, as an international community, had Afghanistan with its 1200 AD mentality rather than contemporary Afghanistan. It would be much easier to reach a peaceful solution in Afghanistan in 1200 AD than in Afghanistan at the moment.

Rural Afghanistan, in fact, currently the most prominent TRME in the globe, was the primary front of the international community against extremism for roughly 15 years. The CF in rural Afghanistan tried to apply Counterinsurgency (COIN) strategies to address the insurgency. Although there emerged a vast literature on the COIN

---

11 Thomas Barfield, "Is Afghanistan 'Medieval'" *Foreign Policy*, (2 June 2010). Full text: <http://www.foreignpolicy.com/articles/2010/06/02/is_afghanistan_medieval> (accessed 15 August 2010).
12 Ibid.
13 Ibid.

strategies of the CF in rural Afghanistan and the prospective policies of the donor countries, unfortunately we have still lacked reliable information about the motivations, aspirations and ideas of the residents of rural Afghanistan, which means that we are still unable to see the other side of the COIN. To some degree, mainly due to the absence of security and inhospitable conditions in Afghanistan, this gap in the literature is understandable. Nonetheless, without knowing the answers to the following questions, we are unable to predict the trend of the war in rural Afghanistan since 'countering an insurgency begins with understanding the complex environment and the numerous competing forces within it'.[14] What is the degree of the *popular base* of the Taliban in rural Afghanistan and is this popular base increasing or decreasing? For instance, what is the tendency of the numbers of intelligence tips flowing from locals to the Afghan National Security Forces, a good indicator of popular support? Are tips increasing or decreasing? Is the recruitment for the Taliban waning or increasing? Are the dead bodies of Taliban members being buried by their families when the dark falls with shame, or buried during the daytime with the participation of thousands and with emotional ceremonies? Are the insurgents seen by locals as aliens or are they local '*sons and nephews?*' What is the fighting strategy of the Taliban? Where are they deploying their members; to their own districts and villages or to the other territories? What does the insurgency mean for the locals in rural Afghanistan? How many Taliban members are surrendering to the Security Forces voluntarily? How do the locals, specifically their families, treat these defectors? Has there been an attempt to implement a general amnesty or rehabilitation program for them?

At first glance, these may be unfamiliar questions for most readers. These are, in fact, tactical level questions, the answers to which are directly related to the end state of the insurgency. Is the good guys winning or losing the insurgency in Afghanistan? To reformulate it, how do we measure 'success' in an insurgency? Which one of these is the best indicator of the success in an insurgency: the number of killed and captured insurgents, the number of killed CF soldiers, the number of attacks conducted by insurgents, the number of missions conducted by the COIN forces, the number of engagements initiated by the Security Forces, the number of civilians protected from insurgents, or the size of areas controlled by the Security Forces? The answers of these questions might seem irrelevant for us as we follow Afghanistan as an interesting foreign policy issue.

So, the overall objective of this book is to draw attention to the conventional COIN strategies currently being applied in TRMEs, and to challenge traditional COIN wisdom available in the literature.

For instance, 'the dilemma of strategic inputs and tactical outcomes' in rural Afghanistan is worth mentioning. In current military thought, modern militaries have three levels of analysis to address any phenomenon they face. First is the tactical level, the lowest level of planning which involves small units ranging from individual

---

14 *FM 3-24 COIN Manual* (2006), pp.2-3.

soldier, squad, and platoon to company. Any issue below the level of battalion, the military unit which involves roughly 600 soldiers and may control an area up to 10 × 10 miles or a town with the population of 5,000, is regarded as a tactical issue. Second is the operational level, which involves units ranging from battalion to brigade, even in some cases division (10,000 soldiers). Third is the strategic level, which is concerned with the overall means and plan for achieving a long-term outcome.

In traditional military thinking, the operational level is considered as the intermediate level in which the aim is to convert the strategy (highest level) into tactics (lowest level of planning). In traditional terms, the operational level, therefore, is considered as the most important level when planning COIN. The battalion or brigade size units are, thus, assumed to be the core units in any planning at the strategic and operational level.

Tactical issues, which are in fact directly related to the execution of the operations, are often skipped since by the military planners they are assumed to be standardized through routine practices, which the military calls Standardized Operational Procedures (SOPs). SOPs often offer guidance where the planning in the operational and strategic level does not cover a situation, or treats a situation only in extremely broad terms. Put simply, in conventional warfare any military commander dealing with planning at the strategic or operational level presupposes that the individual soldier, team, squad and platoon – the units of tactical level – know how to conduct offensive and defensive operations, how to maneuver and engage with the enemy, how and when to shoot, and how and when to engage with civilians. The members of any tactical unit typically promulgate these SOPs based on their experience and specific characteristics of the campaign and the theater.

Where an operational plan exists, SOPs will usually, at least in general terms, adhere to the plan. In the operational plan, commanders provide subordinates a mission, their commander's intent, resources adequate to accomplish it, and a broad conceptual framework which highlights what the mission is and how to fulfill it in general terms. The plan leaves 'details' of execution to subordinates at the tactical level, and expects them to use initiative and judgment to accomplish the mission.

On the other hand, when faced with the dilemmas at the tactical level, junior leaders in the field are habitually inclined to regard strategic or operational plans as 'inaccurate', 'outmoded', 'intricate', or 'insufficient', and thus, ignore them when executing the COIN. Here one may notice that there has always been an inherent gap between the strategic plans and tactical level facts on the ground. The devil is, however, in details, which emerge in this gap in the business of COIN. I would suggest that the capacity of tactical leaders to be able to decode these details, not the strategic plans of senior leaders, will determine whether a COIN force will win or not. In other words, the efficiency of execution at the tactical level will determine the end state in the COIN, not strategic or operational planning.

Therefore, this book challenges traditional COIN strategies, which excessively emphasize 'what to do' in strategic and operational level planning, and it suggests that 'how to do' in tactical level planning is more important to determine the end state of COIN in any TRME.

Similarly, COIN in TRMEs, by nature, is a type of unconventional warfare that cannot be addressed with operational and strategic level planning and that cannot be standardized with SOPs. Every insurgency is unique because of the motivation of the insurgents, historical and cultural facts, terrain and weather conditions, the features of Host Government, and many more *sui generis* dynamics. Units at the tactical level cannot apply the SOPs, which, in fact, embody the institutional inclination to wage conventional warfare with established frameworks. Thus, any tactical unit, which is doomed to be stuck between irrelevant SOPs and inaccurate, insufficient, outmoded, or intricate plans, should develop its own way of implementing COIN, which leads to an inherent 'diversification' at the execution.

Though modern militaries have highly technological command/control and communications capabilities to facilitate the oversight of the senior leadership, the unique characteristics of the COIN in TRMEs – the best example is the one in rural Afghanistan – make oversight barely possible. This low level of oversight and varying features of the COIN theaters accelerate the diversification. The easiest way for a tactical unit in the field is either to apply tactical adaption and innovation in combating the enemy or imitate 'the archive', or what they've learnt from the units they are replacing. The latter option of following the footsteps of their predecessors has always been the preferable alternative when searching for a solution at the tactical level in COIN since it enables less risky and less exhausting solutions. After three or more rotations, the previously diversified procedures in the execution turn out to be 'dogmas' which must be followed unquestioningly. Any innovation is considered risky and assumed as a threat to the security of unit personnel. This cocoon-like way of life at the tactical level highly hinders implementing the pillar of 'learn and adapt', the very basic imperative of COIN in execution at the tactical level.

I wonder if the owners of the boots on the ground in Afghanistan have had concrete, sound and reliable tactical plans derived from strategic directives and operational plans? Could the junior leaders in the field clearly and correctly read the intentions of their commanders when executing operations? If they ignored the plans by blaming them as out-of-date, inadequate or incorrect, did they have SOPs to win the hearts and minds of the locals, or every junior leader implements his/her own style? Did they have SOPs when engaging locals, for instance, or leading a local *jirga*, in a remote village in the middle of nowhere in rural Afghanistan, or playing the mediator role between fighting *Shia* and *Sunni* fractions? Or did they implement their own methods?

Winning and losing at the tactical level

As a person in the business of execution, I would suggest that, the *'organizational capacity'* of the Coalition Forces at the tactical level in Afghanistan was less than what was required to acquire tactical superiority against the insurgents. Interestingly, this deficiency has not been fully addressed in the literature about Afghanistan. We may invest billions of dollars and send thousands of soldiers to the area of theater, but what about the *'outcome' of these efforts* at the tactical level. The tactical level is by far the most important – though the most forgotten level when analyzing the current COIN efforts in rural Afghanistan. That is why my level of analysis will be tactical throughout this book. While some in the US conducted dull discussions on the strategic inputs into the theater of Afghanistan, neither President Obama nor this or that general, but the '*organizational capacity of the CF soldiers at the tactical level*' could win or lose the war in rural Afghanistan. Unfortunately, neither the current literature I reviewed on COIN, including the famous *FM 3-24 Counterinsurgency Manual*, the bible of COIN whose free army-published online version has been downloaded by over two million people,[15] nor the current procedures practiced in the US military, provided clear, concrete and simple answers to remove the question marks which existed in the minds of the soldiers of tactical units on how to conduct COIN in rural Afghanistan. For this reason, the foot soldiers at the tactical level, with many question marks and foggy areas in their minds, were currently trying to fulfill the mission they derive from the situation, 'fighting for their lives and counting down days'.

Another dilemma when tailoring COIN strategies in TRMEs is the excessive reliance on conventional military doctrines. For instance, the idea of the enemy-centric approach has been the starting point of theorizing the doctrines of modern armies, and eventually it has been the foundation of military strategy, force structuring, and military training for decades. This Clausewitzian enemy-centric strategy has become the core principle around which modern armies are built. When conventional direct approach applied to the COIN, the focal assumption is that COIN forces should find, isolate and focus its killing power on the insurgents' decisive point. The hot debates on the US military missions in Afghanistan in the fall of 2009, in fact, revitalized the conventional enemy-centric approach. The strategy of reducing the US involvement in the nation-building efforts and ramping up drone attacks and covert raids against high-profile al-Qaeda targets in Pakistan's tribal areas, which was first proposed by Vice President Joe Biden, is a perfect case for this approach. *The New York Times* highlighted this strategy, the principal rationale of which was to neutralize al-Qaeda members, by reporting that 'rather than trying to protect the Afghan population from the Taliban, American forces would concentrate on strikes against al-Qaeda cells, primarily in Pakistan, using Special Forces, Predator missile attacks, and other surgical tactics'.[16]

I, however, challenge to the objective of the destruction of enemy for a clear victory in TRMEs, and suggest that the support of the populace should be the center of gravity. Therefore, to insist on conceptualizing the insurgency in TRMEs as a deviation of traditional Clausewitzian war, where two antagonists each endeavor to impose their will on and crush the opponent in pursuit of political objectives, does

---

15   *Chicago Tribune*, (8 September 2007).
16   Peter Barker and Elisabeth Bumiller, 'Obama considers a strategy shift in Afghan War' *The New York Times*, (22 September 2010). Full text: <http://www.nytimes.com/2009/09/23/world/asia/23policy.html> (accessed 1 September 2010).

not conform to today's reality. In other words, fully acknowledging that war is always fought for political purposes – that war is nothing but the continuation of politics by other means, I am inclined to suggest that not all armed conflict in contemporary security environments does mean war. Though I do not underestimate the importance of kinetic conventional capabilities to achieve success, the battle between the COIN forces and the insurgents in TRMEs is, in fact, a struggle for gaining the recognition of the populace. Stated another way, without achieving an acceptable level of approval and support of the local populace by applying population-centric approaches, it is merely possible to establish a secure and stable environment for the locals, the primary objective of the COIN in the TRMEs. Nonetheless, the objective of gaining the support of the population should not be reduced to 'winning hearts and minds'. That is, being kind to the locals, meeting their material needs and making them feel grateful to you does not necessarily mean that they stop supporting insurgents. In TRMEs, one may find roughly all hearts and minds for rent, but not surely all for sale since they have been reserved by the traditional mechanism that has governed TRMEs for centuries.

Getting beyond 'Islamic radicalism'

Another emphasis of this book is to remove the veil of 'Islamic radicalism' on the current fight in tribalized and rural Afghanistan and many TRMEs in the globe. To facilitate this aim, one should conduct a sort of morphological analysis of a typical TRME, for instance rural Afghanistan, at the tactical level.

We had plenty of discussion sessions on TRMEs in classes with many American officers from all branches during my education in the US, a great majority of whom served in the TRMEs of Afghanistan and Iraq at least one time, most of whom even served multiple times. Sadly, a very few of them fully understand what is going on in rural Afghanistan at the tactical level. I recalled that I was the first student who raised his hand and talked about the impacts of tribal characteristics on COIN efforts in rural Afghanistan after two hours of discussion on Afghanistan in a room filled with more than 40 junior-level US officers from all forces. We were discussing radical Islam, the notion of *Jihad*, al-Qaeda, and all religious phenomena coming with the package of radical Islam until that time. As it transpired in this session, and in many of the classes in which I participated, the main theme had always been the radical Islam and it was often cited first. An ordinary American citizen in the US may prefer to use 'Islamic' as an adjective in front of the insurgency in Afghanistan and may not need any other adjective, which could be excused to some extent since they could not find a chance to see what is really happening in rural Afghanistan with their own eyes. On the other hand, if roughly all junior-level officers I met in the US military, who also served in Afghanistan or Iraq at least one time at the tactical level, are inclined to put radical Islam as an adjective to define the insurgency in Afghanistan and if they mention nothing else but for Islam, then, I would suggest that there is an 'institutional' problem in the diagnosis phase.

First, excessive emphasis of the phenomena coming in the package of radical Islam in the US military education system functions as a veil which covers all other phenomena highly relevant for the COIN efforts in Afghanistan. Any US soldier in rural Afghanistan is, thus, inclined to fall into the fallacy of putting Islam as an adjective in front of any socio-cultural, political, security-related or economic issue he/she is faced with. The explanatory power of radical Islam is unprecedented for many US soldiers when it comes to explain any dilemma in rural Afghanistan. The understanding of 'it is because of Islam, that is all folks' seems to cover all relevant phenomena. This inclination to explain everything with a single root cause leads many US soldiers to fall into 'the single factor fallacy'. The military education system, in fact, should be designed to challenge the media-driven stereotypes, which reinforce the phenomenon of 'Islamic radicalism' among a Western audience.

Second, mainly because of the nirvana fallacy of 'force protection' and current risk-averse method of operating, the US soldiers in Afghanistan have highly limited access to 'real locals' – not the pseudo ones such as interpreters or local contractors who say what the US soldiers want to hear. Therefore, to get first-hand information, which may disrupt their pre-conditionings and biases through experience/observation is excessively unlikely for any US soldier. I personally know many junior-level officers who could not see 'a real Afghan', though they spent more than six months in Afghanistan. When the political cost of a fallen soldier outweighs the risks of interacting with the locals to be acquainted with the environment – one of the imperatives of COIN, the result for any US soldier is to 'visualize' rural Afghanistan through what he/she learnt from the indoctrination before the deployment and through what he/she heard from others during the deployment.

There are some, however, who could remove the veil of radical Islam a little and could figure out the importance of the dynamics other than Islam, such as the tribal structures in TRMEs. Unfortunately, though they spent some time in TRMEs and closely experienced the importance of tribal characteristics, they are, fatally, inclined to recognize tribal order as the sole player and measure power in material terms in TRMEs. Major Jim Gant states in his report, 'One Tribe at a Time', that 'Money and guns equal the ultimate power' in TRMEs.[17] He continues that 'power in this area [in TRMEs] was about the ability to put armed men on the ground to attack an adversary or to defend the tribe. Guns were the ultimate currency'.[18]

As a 'hard-head' Special Forces soldier, his argument could be seen accurate at first glance. I, however, would suggest that the power rooted from the 'money and gun' strategy could foster temporary solutions on particular issues in specific part of TRMEs, but cannot cultivate a stable, permanent, cohesive and comprehensive end state. The end state of the reliance on material powers such as money and arms

---

17 Full report: <http://rohrabacher.house.gov/UploadedFiles/one_tribe_at_a_time.pdf> (accessed 17 August 2010).
18 Ibid.

to mobilize specifically selected tribes or individuals against a common enemy is warlordism, the symbiotic relationship of which with the Taliban, in fact, feeds the current chaos in Afghanistan. Any strategy, the reference point of which is not 'the superstructure', which will be proposed in this book as the main source of legitimization that revolves the TRMEs, is null and void. Or simply put, any 'materialistic or mechanical' strategy that cannot satisfy the mental and emotive component of TRMEs, or a strategy with no 'soul', is doomed to fail sooner or later.

Understanding TRMEs

Tribalized, rural and Muslim Afghanistan is a highly complex and significant environment, though rarely studied from COIN perspective. The utmost aim of this book is to propose a new approach which endeavors to address the core issues regarding the COIN efforts in rural Afghanistan. This is not a problem-solving book. It may be regarded, instead, as a book of problem-setting at the tactical level and concerning the TRMEs in general. That is why it attacks many 'dogmas' currently existing in the COIN literature. It claims that the current situation in rural Afghanistan does not conform to established frames or assumptions in the literature, and the current literature is, thus, far behind from figuring out what the real problem is.

For instance, the word 'government' is used 105 times in *FM 3-24*. According to the manual, the primary objective of any COIN operation is to foster development of effective governance by a legitimate government.'[19] Then, we may assert that rural Afghanistan should be categorized as an ungoverned territory because of the absence of the notion of the state or the existence of the state capacity, or because the state faces significant challenges in establishing control.

The Rand Report describes ungovernability through four variables:

1. the level of state penetration of society
2. the extent to which the state has a monopoly on the use of force
3. the extent to which the state controls its borders
4. whether the state is subject to external intervention by other states[20]

Presumably, then, the remedy for the current ungovernability in rural Afghanistan would be to increase the interaction of the state with rural society, to strengthen the monopoly of the state over the use of violence to control and stabilize its claimed territory and borders, and to increase the legitimacy of the state in the eyes of its population and the sovereignty of the state in the international system. These state-centric solutions might be valid for territories where the population understands the notion

---

19 *FM 3-24*, pp.1-21.
20 The Rand Report, 'Ungoverned Territories' (Santa Monica, CA: Rand Cooperation, 2007). <http://www.rand.org/pubs/monographs/MG561/> (accessed 27 June 2009).

of a state. In developed states, the actions of consolidating and monopolizing the legitimate right to use violence, providing security against internal/external threats, policing activities and justice, extracting resources from the population and territory, and creating institutions for the benefit of the population are naturally carried out by the state. The primary objective of any COIN strategy in rural Afghanistan should, therefore, consolidate the state capacity.

In contrast, I would suggest that rural Afghanistan and many TRMEs in the globe are not ungoverned. In fact, they have been governed territories for centuries, but with governance models different from state-centric. With particular focus on Afghanistan, defining TRMEs from a state-centric approach and excessive emphasis on the notion of government when tailoring COIN efforts would be misleading and will fall short of accurately addressing current dynamics in these troubled regions. That is, since the notion of state has not yet dawned in the minds of the residents of those territories, any state-centric approach to address the current dynamics in TRMEs would probably lead to false conclusions.

Defining security

Another fallacy of the traditional COIN literature is the excessive emphasis of the notion of 'security'. *FM 3-24*, in which the word 'security' is used 137 times, asserts that 'the cornerstone of any COIN effort is establishing security for civilian populace'[21] and concludes that 'no permanent reforms can be implemented and disorder spreads'[22] without a secure environment. The manual also regards 'the ability to provide security for the populace' as the first indicator of legitimacy.[23] Then, security should be the primary concern in any COIN effort in TRMEs, specifically in rural Afghanistan. I, however, am inclined to think differently. Security may be one of the imperatives of any COIN in TRMEs, nonetheless, considering it as the first and utmost objective which should be obsessively achieved, may lead any COIN strategy to a wrong direction.

The notion of 'freedom' is the primary value associated with Western civilization when defining the relation between the individual and governing political entity or the state. It is only the notion of 'justice', the primary value associated with TRMEs, that can only give enough legitimacy to govern in the people's eyes, particularly if they have experienced a serious breakdown of order. Justice is a 'glue' that binds all features of any TRME and orders the society. Put simply, it is much more important to be 'justly' treated than to be 'secured' for the residents of TRMEs. If so, 'Hi guys, we are here to establish the state authority, but we should secure you first' strategy is totally an alien concept for locals, and thus, presumably may attract less support than the strategy of '*Esselamun Aleykum ihvan-i muslimin*' (May peace of God be upon you

---

21 *FM 3-24*, pp.1-23.
22 Ibid, pp.1-23.
23 Ibid, pp.1-21.

fellow Muslims), we are here to establish a *just* social order and aim to clean the environment from all earthly sins you currently suffer.'

The primary concern of anyone in any TRME is less corruption – as the more preferably solution, or more chance to participate in it – as the less preferable solution. To reformulate it, the residents of TRMEs either seek for a just social order, in which they would share 'misery' equally as long as it is a just solution, or seek for an unequal share of wealth, which is an unjust solution as long as they could exploit it. While the former concept is represented by the Taliban in rural Afghanistan, the latter is represented by the corrupted warlord order and the CF-supported government. The reference point in both of these concepts is justice, not security. Any social interaction is evaluated through the lenses of justice in TRMEs. That is why the *badal* or *kisas* rule, a just retaliation which justifies the proportionate use of violence in response to a crime, is a common practice.

Furthermore, with regard to justice, the Western mindset puts 'accuracy' above all other considerations. In the Western world, a methodical and long process to find justice is always appropriate, since the environment provided by the authority of the state is secure enough to await a verdict. The Western mindset demands that the decision of the judge be accurate and objective. In contrast, people in TRMEs seek 'the swift implementation' of justice rather than concern themselves with accuracy, since they do not have enough time and patience to wait.

First, a TRME is an inappropriate setting for a prolonged legal dispute since there is no superior authority to make both sides wait patiently and peacefully for the decision. Second, the uncertain result of any legal issue can cause more destructive consequences in TRMEs than the issue itself, potentially turning a crime into a tribal or interfamily feud, which could last for decades and claim the lives of many adult males. Thus, to reach a decision as soon as possible that would somewhat satisfy each side and avoid inter-tribe or inter-family conflicts is preferable to a lengthy judicial process. In *FM 3-24*, which is full of 'security', the concept of 'rule of law' is only used two times,[24] as a notion to support the argument of achieving legitimacy thorough security. I remember an interesting wish from my childhood commonly used in my village by the people for their loved ones. They say that 'May God bless you a just death'. If a death is considered 'just' in TRMEs, then people welcome it. Put simply, it is the notion of justice that revolves the TRMEs, not the notion of security. The remark of Ali ibn Abi Talib, the son-in-law of Prophet Muhammad, explicitly demonstrates to what extent the notion of justice is important for Muslim societies. 'Government [any political entity] can endure with unbelief, but not with injustice'.[25] In basic terms, security should not be an 'end' when tailoring an effective COIN strategy for TRMEs, it should, instead be a means in the process of the creation of a 'just socio-political order'.

---

24 *FM 3-24*, The first usage is in p.1; the second one is in pp.1-23.
25 Carl W. Ernst, *Following Muhammad: Rethinking Islam in the Contemporary World* (London: University of North Carolina Press, 2003), p.118.

Another dilemma in *FM 3-24* regarding the notion of justice is that it excessively emphasizes on the physical component of security. One of the pillars of the COIN is to separate insurgents from the populace, which, according to *FM 3-24*, necessities cordon and control-based military operations to deny the physical access of insurgents to the locals.[26] This pillar, however, should not be understood solely in physical terms. The other component of security is the emotional and mental one, which is by far more important than the former one but precisely underestimated by current COIN strategies. In behavioral science, value is defined as a socially shared idea about what is 'good', 'right', and 'desirable'. The norm is defined as a shared rule or guideline that prescribes the behavior appropriate in a given situation. Then, the efforts to help the society to secure the correct norms and values against the war on extremism should be of higher importance rather than the physical security of the society itself. Nonetheless, the question of how we would secure the hearts and minds of the locals from the rhetoric of the insurgents is often omitted in the current COIN literature, and the literature by and large focuses on the physical security of the villages, districts and towns. The excessive focus on the material or physical security in the existing COIN literature, which in fact leads to the omission of the mental and emotional component, is therefore worth mentioning as an erroneous effort.

Similar to the security-centric approaches, the emerging talks of paying Afghan tribes to give up violence and start fighting against the Taliban have also been popular so of late among COIN strategists. The pact, or the 'carrot strategy', appeared between the Shinwari tribe in Afghanistan and the CF, which proposed channeling of $1 million in development-based projects directly to the villages of this tribe in exchange for their support in the fight against the Taliban; this has been presented as promising news in the Western media.[27] For Stephen Farrell, this strategy of paying Afghan tribes brings to mind a poem by Rudyard Kipling about the Danegeld, a levy paid in Anglo-Saxon England in an attempt to buy off Danish invaders. The poem says:

> It is always a temptation to rich and lazy nation
> To puff and look important and to say
> Though we know we should defeat you
> We have not the time to meet you
> We will therefore pay you cash to go away[28]

For me this strategy of paying for the tribes, or 'cow-to be milked syndrome' I will call in the subsequent chapters, is futile. In any prolonged fight conducted by wealthy armies such as the CF against any insurgency in a socio-economically deprived,

---

26 *FM 3-24*, pp.1-29.
27 Dexter Filkins, 'Afghan Tribe, Vowing to Fight Taliban to Get US Aid Return', *The New York Times* (28 January 2010).
28 Stephen Farrell, 'Pay You Cash to Go Away', *The New York Times* (28 January 2010).

highly isolated and primitive environment such as rural Afghanistan, there emerges a very simple question. Who is the real exploiter of the continuation of the conflict? The CF is not only a highly valuable target but also highly valuable asset in economic terms for the locals. For the people in rural Afghanistan, the corrupted warlord order and government institutions which benefit by aligning with the CF, represent the rhetoric of more chance to participate in corruption. I do not use the term 'corruption' in a negative sense here; instead, I use it to define the unjust economic exploitation of the presence of the foreigners in Afghanistan. The conflict, at least in the local level, will turn out to be a fierce and brutal fighting between the happy minority, who have benefited from the economic and political privileges of being the trusted ones of the CF, and the desperate majority who want nothing but for the *equal share of corruption* flowing from the CF. Consequently, it is likely that every passing year made the corruption circles surrounding the bases of the CF forces thicker, and after passing a certain threshold, it was impossible to decide who was exploiting whom and for what purposes. Who was the real enemy or friend?

Unfortunately, for the ones who have not adequately benefited from these circles, there was another address to go: the Taliban. Sarcastically, if the CF could spread the current *widespread corruption* circling itself to the rest of Afghanistan with equal shares and make everybody in Afghanistan involved in a grand corruption circle, then this could be claimed a clear victory.

In conclusion, this book is a means to conceptualize and hypothesize about the underlying causes that explain the phenomenon of TRMEs, still an unfamiliar one for many. It also aims to lay out a different perspective regarding the COIN efforts in rural areas at the tactical level, a rarely-studied field.

Though I am fully aware that one man's account cannot be taken as the facts, I, as a person who spent his childhood in a remote village perfectly fits for the definition of TRME; I offer my observation on the basis of 10 years of field experience in rural Iraq, Turkey, Kazakhstan, Kyrgyzstan and Afghanistan. Although limited to five states, I believe that my experience may point to some general characteristics of TRMEs and COIN efforts at the tactical level to factilitate the objectives of the book.

The first chapter focuses on what tribalized, rural and Muslim environment means. It analyzes the moral codes of behaviors that have ruled TRMEs for centuries. It also lays out the political, socio-cultural and economic aspects of TRMEs, and describes the underpinning reasons of the current conflict in rural Afghanistan. This chapter specifically aims to present the delicate equilibrium in TRMEs, which is based on the amalgamation of modified Islam, (used to meet the tasks of regulating socio-economic life) with traditional tribal codes, *urf ad'at* or *tore*, idealized as the wisdom of past generations. It is this established normative framework, or moral codes of behavior, (or *akhlaq* in Arabic) which is revered by everybody in TRMEs and used in the handling of all social relations since it meets every political, religious, and socio-economic demand in the daily life of the tribal order. This chapter also explains the definition of the institutional mechanism, or 'the superstructure', that facilitates the implementation of moral codes of behavior, and thus defines the way of life in the TRMEs.

The second chapter, 'Afghanistan: The View from the Ground', analyzes the antecedent conditions of the current turmoil and addresses many ongoing dilemmas in rural Afghanistan. This chapter also presents a morphological analysis of rural Afghanistan and addresses many vital issues raised by the COIN strategies of the CF at the tactical level in rural Afghanistan.

The third chapter, 'The Other Side of the COIN', aims to draw attentions to the execution of COIN through tactical-level analysis. The overall question this chapter seeks to answer is that when we put tribal structures, rural environments and Islam into a blender and blend them, which sort of outcomes are we likely to face in political, socio-cultural and economic terms and will those outcomes effect COIN efforts in Afghanistan?

The last chapter is the conclusion, which emphasizes why we need more military designing to set the stage accurately in TRMEs like rural Afghanistan, but not military planning to solve the problems confronted with pre-existing cognitive templates. In this sense, military designing, or the process of conceptualizing; defining and describing the nature and characteristics of the security environment at hand, should be the very first step of any military effort in low intensity conflict environments.

1

What is Tribalized Rural Muslim Environment (TRME)?

Would You Die For Your Backyard?

Imagine this scenario for a moment. You wake up on a sunny Sunday morning, eager to eat breakfast with your family. However, you hear strange noises coming from your backyard. When you step outside to see what is going on, the bizarre scene you witness shocks you. A group of foreigners are trying to settle in your backyard. You also notice that some of these scary people are armed, although there are women and children among them. They do not look friendly, and they look like they intend to stay for a long time.

How would you react to this provocative scene? Call 911? Unfortunately, there is no response. You call the local police, but again no response. To reach your neighbors or somebody in the street would be a good idea but, unfortunately, you can't see anybody nearby. You tell your family to stay upstairs. Should you try to communicate with the foreigners and explain that the land that they are trying to settle is your backyard? You open the door to the backyard and yell at those people without saying 'hi' since this is not a friendly visit. In fact it is an occupation of land which belongs to you.

'What are you doing in my backyard?' An elderly man in the group, presumably their leader, answers your question politely. 'This a lovely land, on which we decided to settle and pass the summer with our families. Besides, who says this is your back yard?' Then he commences to encircle the area with a fence.

How would you act under these circumstances? Accustomed to receiving security services from the state since you were born, you suddenly have to provide security for yourself and for your loved ones in your house, and for your property. Should you negotiate and seek a compromise since the elder in the group looks honorable and trustworthy? Would a compromise to share half of your backyard with these occupiers be a viable option? But the fact continues to be that this has been your backyard since you were born! Besides, how would your family react when they hear that you, desperately and cowardly, accepted to share half of your backyard with those occupiers?

At this point, there seems to be only one option open to you, to scare the foreigners away. You remember that you have a gun somewhere in your house. In the absence of a state to protect you, the use of a weapon would be justified since nobody, including your family, will blame you for applying violence. You are honorably trying to defend your property and the future of your children.

You find your rifle, load it and turn back to your yard to threaten those foreigners into leaving. Before the confrontation you ask yourself if there is anybody who can come to help you. Surely an ally and another rifle would make you more persuasive. If your answer is 'no' then you may feel some regret that you have lived such an individualistic way of life. Had you had a number of friends to call, who would be willing to die for your backyard with you, you would have had a better chance against the foreigners. Still, you take comfort in knowing that if you lose this armed confrontation and are killed, everybody will remember you as an honorable man who gave his life for his loved ones, property and the values he believed in.

One last question: if things do not go well, and you decide to use your rifle, will you shoot only at the armed men in the group or will you shoot, indiscriminately, to kill them all, including the women and children in the group? If you only aim to kill armed men, this would be honorable behavior, but when you leave the rest, specifically other unarmed men and their sons, they would come after you and your family, which means turning this confrontation in to a bloody and years-long feud. Moreover, if you get killed in this challenge, are you entirely sure that the occupiers will let your family leave from the house peacefully?

This scenario is completely hypothetical for many people, who currently live within a state. That is, for us, that state is defined as a political entity which:

a) consolidates the monopoly over the legitimate right to use violence within a pre-defined territory;
b) provides security against internal/external threats;
c) conducts policing activities;
d) possesses the right to extract resources from the population and territory it controls;
e) creates institutions for the material benefits of the population living in this pre-defined territory.

State, in the modern sense, provides all these services stated above. By the same token, this is a true story for many others, who happen to be born in remote parts of states where there is no effective state authority. There are many rural territories in the world, in which the notion of state and all the faculties provided by the state are elusive.

Some Western experts assert that TRMEs in many parts of rural Afghanistan should be categorized as *ungoverned*[1] territories because of the absence of the notion

---

1   The Rand Report, 'Ungoverned Territories' (Santa Monica: Rand Cooperation, 2007). <http://www.rand.org/pubs/monographs/MG561/> (accessed 27 June 2009).

of state or the existence of state capacity, or because the state faces significant challenges in establishing control. In contrast, I argue that TRMEs in these countries are not ungoverned. In fact, they have been governed territories for centuries, but with governance models different than state-centric. With particular focus on Afghanistan, I argue that defining TRMEs from a state-centric approach would be misleading and will fall short of accurately addressing current dynamics in these troubled regions.

For example, the Rand Report describes ungovernability through four variables:

1. the level of state penetration of society;
2. the extent to which the state has a monopoly on the use of force;
3. the extent to which the state controls its borders;
4. whether the state is subject to external intervention by other states.[2]

Presumably then, the remedy for the current ungovernability in TRMEs would be to increase the interaction of the state with rural society, to strengthen the monopoly of the state over the use of violence to control and stabilize its claimed territory and borders, and to increase the legitimacy of the state in the eyes of its population and the sovereignty of the state in the international system. These state-centric solutions might be valid for territories where the population understands the notion of a state. In developed states, the actions of consolidating and monopolizing the legitimate right to use violence, providing security against internal/external threats, policing activities and justice, extracting resources from the population and territory, and creating institutions for the benefit of the population are naturally carried out by *the state*.[3]

But are these functions of the state also valid for geographically isolated, socioeconomically deprived, materially primitive and totally pastoral societies currently living in TRMEs within the remote parts of Afghanistan? Since the notion of state has not yet dawned in the minds of the residents of those territories, any state-centric approach to address the current dynamics in TRMEs would likely lead to false conclusions. Instead these dynamics revolve around the tribal order.[4] In contrast, in TRMEs it is the tribal order that facilitates these services. Therefore neither any state-centric approach cannot accurately address any issue in TRMEs nor can the imposition of a purely state-centric solution can effectively resolve any structural problem in TRMEs. The particular characteristics of the TRMEs may vary, while the general characteristics of the TRMEs are the same regardless of time and space.

---

2   Ibid, p.xvi.
3   Cynthia H. Enloe and Mostafa Rejai, 'Nation-states and State-Nations', *International Studies Quarterly No 13*, No.2 (Jun 1969), 140-158, p.140.
4   Video clip of Ismail Khan, the ruler of Herat province in Afghanistan and the legendary Mujahidin commander who rebelled against the Soviet Invasion on 16 March 1979. His handling of the governance and delivery of the justice, more importantly the obedience of the people to his authority are worth mentioning in this YouTube video: <http://www.youtube.com/watch?v=_rsv1RyI1w0> (accessed 7 September 2009).

In this chapter, I will present the general characteristics of the TRMEs. I should stress one last note before beginning. As emphasized when explaining the notion of justice in the introduction, Western ideas of what is 'normal' or 'rational' are not universal. In contrast, other societies often have different notions of; rationality, appropriate moral codes of behavior, level of religious devotion, and value systems concerning many facets of socio-cultural life. Thus, what may appear 'abnormal' or 'peculiar' to an outsider may appear as self-evidently normal to a particular society. For this reason, one should strive to avoid imposing his/her ideals of normalcy on any issue regarding TRMEs. Gender issues in TRMEs – specifically gloomy news that the Western audience read/watch in Western media regarding the severe restrictions on women's behavior – could be a good example to indicate primitiveness and savageness of the TRMEs when looked through the lenses of the Western value system. However, the *namus* concept which has been both religiously and traditionally justified, dictates that the sexual integrity and dignity of a woman, specifically an unmarried young lady, is not only her individual matter but also the matter of whole extended family, even tribe. According to this concept, the family/tribe should protect the chastity and social dignity of all women in the family/tribe against all kinds of physical and verbal threats. All women in a family/tribe represent the honor and reputation of that particular family/tribe. Sexual integrity of women is, thus, not a personal but a social phenomenon. The *namus* concept provides a collective security umbrella for each woman in the system. It regulates that all women, who feel the power of the family/tribe name behind their back, can travel safely, conduct daily routines at home or the in fields and establish social contacts with other individuals safely in the TRMEs, in which state-imposed laws are irrelevant. By means of this concept, women are also totally excluded from any form of punishment in inter-tribe/family disputes. Women can also neither be interrogated nor be put in prison for any crime. I observed personally many times that a group of female villagers – only accompanied by an old man – would go to the pastoral fields, which are miles away from the village, for agricultural work and would stay there safely for days. Also, on numerous occasions, I encountered female shepherds in the mountains who roam there for days safely with their livestock. That is why the Western audiences, who have been bombarded with the news about the Taliban's treatment of women and the Taliban's gender policies, would falsely conclude that the *namus* concept, which is in fact manipulated by the Taliban, is extremely primitive and wild, and should be challenged in every medium. Let me ask this question. We all have seen at least one picture of an Afghan lady who wears a dress called *burqa*, or *chadri* that covers the wearer's entire face except for a small region of the eyes, which is covered by a concealing net. Is the practice of wearing *burqa* or *chadri*, a religious or a traditional one? And are the women in Afghanistan wearing them against their will or voluntarily? According to the current literature available for Western audience, women are forced to wear the *burqa* in public by the Taliban as the proper dress code of *Sharia* Law. Because, according to a Taliban spokesman, 'the face of a woman is a source of corruption' for men.⁵ A Taliban decree from 1996 also states, 'if women are going outside with fashionable, ornamental, tight and charming clothes to show themselves, they will be cursed by the Islamic *Sharia*, and should never expect to go to heaven'.⁶ Then one may conclude that the practice of wearing a *burqa* is an imposed religious code by the Taliban for women in Afghanistan. Fully agreeing that the fear from the Taliban and religious motives would be a cause of wearing of *burqa* for many ladies in TRMEs, I would suggest that this is not necessarily true for all cases. I have been told by many ladies in TRMEs that they wear the *burqa* or *burqa*-like dresses voluntarily and for security reasons. That is, in an insecure environment in which they could be harassed, kidnapped or even raped, to cover their bodies wholly is the sole option to reduce their public visibility and thus not to attract too much attention. Some of them, interestingly, complained about the waning power of moral codes of behaviors, including the *namus* concept in their societies. Then, I came to conclude that firstly, there is a direct correlation between the prevalence of perceived insecurity in a given society and the dress preferences of women. And secondly, the *namus* concept should not be solely defined as a religious phenomenon but also may be defined as a traditionally instituted social phenomenon which has kept women in safety for centuries in TRMEs. I would also conclude that by means of relatively modern phenomena, which have emerged in the TRMEs (such as warlordism, modern criminal networks, and corrupted state-governed legal systems) pump insecurity into the environment – and thus women – are willing to be under the security umbrella of the *namus* concept. Nonetheless, in a TRME the social equilibrium of which is drastically imbalanced with exogenous inputs, and as a poor and powerless father of a young lady, how would you act in accordance with the *namus* concept if your daughter has been kidnapped by a local warlord? And to what extent would this concept deter this ill-intentioned local warlord?

Tribal Rural Muslim Environments

Tribal order is a particular form of socio-economic and political control that completely rejects other belief systems introduced by the *outsiders* into the traditional way of life. Tribal order does not simply reject novelty; it actively demands constant lifestyle correction according to an ancient, primordial ethos. The only important thing is that society in the tribal order must not depart from the ideal form.

---

5   M. J. Gohari, *The Taliban: Ascent to Power* (Oxford: Oxford University Press, 2001), pp.108-110.
6   Allen Nacheman, 'Afghan women tell tales of brutality, terror at hands of Taliban', *Agence France Press* (2001). <http://www.webcitation.org/query?url=http://www.geocities.com/CapitolHill/Parliament/1358/talibans-graphic-stories.html&date=2009-10-25+10:32:35> (accessed 26 September 2010).

I encounter in literature several times that there is an inclination to regard that the tribal order and the European feudal system as similar concepts. The society in TRMEs is, in fact, fundamentally different from European feudal society. In feudalism the land is distributed by the king with the royal authority to the chief. The chief (or lord) leases some parts of his lands to the other 'estates' such as knights, and knights assign their granted land to the middle level farmers to cultivate.[7] Feudalism, a predominantly static and top-to-bottom social structure which gives rise to a hierarchy of rank, and is characterized by classes of militarized landholders and working landless peasants. The loyalty of those peasants to a specific lord is assigned and legitimized by the royal authority. The lord is expected to protect and provide justice and essential services to those landless peasants. Only the personal bonds based on an oath of allegiance bind the peasants temporarily to the lord, and those bonds must be renewed with a new lord.[8] It is also worth noting that the Catholic Church, which enabled the institutionalization and bureaucratization of Christianity, was an essential part of feudalism since it was one of the biggest landowners, thus a ruler, in Europe.

In contrast to feudalism, a tribesman in rural Iraq or Afghanistan has been always free and not forcibly bound to the land. Land has been under the control of his tribe, and so is his property. He could sell the land that belonged to him, or leave, with the consent of the tribal elders. Moreover, the most fertile lands that include water resources and permanent pastures for the livestock are in collective ownership and the control of the tribe – even if these lands are frequently the cause of inter-family and inter-tribal feuds.

Tribal order, based on kinship and blood ties, is a bottom-to-top social structure. A leadership position in TRMEs is not an assigned but to some extent elected position, legitimized by all members in the order, including the religious leaders, since a consensus among the people on the legitimacy of the leader enables him to lead. Any leadership position not legitimized by tribal consent, for instance, if a leader tries to use force to accelerate the legitimization process, is not so powerful and likely to cause aggravation. Moreover, since the legitimization of the leader is granted by his own people in the tribe, in contrast to the feudalism in which the legitimization is granted by the king, it is vital for the leader to focus on the internal dynamics of the tribal order so as to please his voluntary followers. Thus, the intra-tribe dynamics necessitate active participation of leaders with tribal members in order to govern.

Tribe vs State

Whereas the predominant unit of social organization in a state is the *nation*, this predominant unit in TRMEs is the *tribe*. The citizen in the state is a constitutionally

---

7 Hagen Schulze States, *Nation and Nationalism* (Malden: Blackwell Publishers, 1994), p.6.
8 Ibid, p.7.

autonomous and free individual, possessing a legal right to determine his/her destiny and pursue personal preferences within the framework rule of law. In contrast, the tribesman in the tribal order is a proud member of a group. He or she has a strong sense of belonging and a sense of mission derived from being a part of something greater than one's self.

The tribes, commonly named as *ashira, qabila, taifa, tira, oba, hawz, asiret* in TRMEs, are not easy to define since their; sizes, structures, internal organizations and interactions with the outside world significantly vary. But the dominant tribal pattern in any TRME is based upon a good blend of kinship ideology and socialized Islam. Such kinship ideology is usually rooted in the sense of common ancestry, which includes the heroes from the pre-Islamic period and even descendants (*sayyids*) of the Prophet Muhammad. The glorification of the past and its ancestral links has been a particularly attractive form of legitimization in TRMEs. Islam also highly celebrates the period of Prophet Muhammad and his friends (*Sahabi*), the succeeding generation who saw them (*tabiin*), and the third generation who saw *tabbins* (*tebe-i tabiin*), and glorifies those three generations for their selfless efforts and sufferings to expand Islam. This, in turn, is one of the primary reasons why Islam is very compatible with the tribal order. Namely, both aim to glorify the *golden age in the past* and the ancestors who lived up to the principles of the superstructure. That is why, tribal leaders aim to legitimize political power and purify kinship by marrying a lady from a respected clerical family – preferably *sayyid* – so as to join the elite club.

In addition, most tribes also possess a strong sense of territorial identity that goes along with the ideas of ancestry. This identity, which may generally be the root cause of the tribal feuds, permeates the villages and recognized territories of the tribe. Any political solution disregarding the fact of territorial identities of the tribes or violating them may be confronted by strong reactions from the tribes. The tribal leader is mainly responsible for maintaining order, applying justice and possibly collecting taxes within this defined territory. David McDowall writes:

> The two systems [state and tribe] seem fundamentally incompatible, their relations at best only temporarily symbiotic. States are static, intent on monopoly of power within a defined territory. They require an urban dimension which embodies a bureaucracy and culture based upon the written word. They comprise a multiplicity of economic legal and administrative functions in town and the country and may include religious functions also. Tribes operate on kinship ideology and territoriality, the latter includes both established villages but also more fluid ideas that no state could entertain. The fundamental reason, however, why states and tribes are incompatible lies with the whole reason of tribal hierarchy. Tribal chiefs at all levels are required to discharge certain functions. Within the group acknowledging their chiefship they act as arbitrators of disputes and allocators of resources, benefits and duties. Beyond the tribal groups, the chief acts as mediators either with his peers and paramount chief, or with the state [central authority]. A chief jealously guards his monopoly of

all relations with the outside world. If a state exercises a monopoly of power, its authority regarding taxation and the administration of justice will extend to every individual within its territory, rendering the mediation of the tribal chief with the outside world.⁹

The political and administrative authority of a strong state extends to every individual within state territory. Then, one does not need the myths of common ancestry and territorial identity if he takes his livestock to pasture, or waters his lands with state-built irrigation systems, or claims ownership with state-given land deeds. If the state, rather than the tribal leader, will provide justice and essential services, then the state would be more successful in bringing tribes under its direct control. Recently this is precisely what has become the conflict between the role of the tribe and the state, raising questions about the compatibility between a tribe and a modern state. Similar to the remarks of McDowall, Henry Walter Bellew (1834-1892), an Indian-born British medical officer and author, explains the dilemma of the compatibility between the tribal order and modern state in the sense of the 'Westphalian' model in Afghanistan by stating that:

> In Afghanistan, tribes predate the creation of the formal state structure in the sense of the 'Westphalian' model. Notwithstanding the evolution of tradition in the presence of Islam, tribal tradition also predates the prevalence of Islam in Afghanistan. Therefore, any attempt by the centralized state to exude authority over the tribes has predictably been resisted; subsequently, control of tribes has been one of the perennial problems of the government. Anthropological studies regarding tribal structures suggest that the state and the tribes are incongruous both in function and structure. As far as the Afghan tribes are concerned, it is state and not tribe which occupy the periphery of things, and it is to the state that all the characteristics of the peripheral attach. In light of this, tribes are perceived by the state as challengers to state authority and utility.¹⁰

Center-periphery relation between state and the rural/tribal order would be characterized by continuous state attempts to make a way into tribal order and impose control; while the tribal and rural institutions have always been averse to state interference in their affairs.

There are some crucial points in understanding this historical friction between center and the periphery. First, there is no clear definition of which entity, state or tribal order, constitutes the periphery. Though for us modern state represents the

---

9   David McDowall, *A Modern History of the Kurds* (New York: St. Martin's Press, 1996), p.14.
10 H.W. Bellow, *Inquiry into the Ethnography of Afghanistan* (Graz, Austria: Akademische druck-u, 1973).

center, people in TRMEs view state as peripheral primarily because state is a relatively young modern creation, and tribal order has existed for centuries solely relying on their own social structure for governance and services; therefore, people in TRMEs see no utility in the existence of a central state.

Furthermore, the perception of state as a non-traditional and un-Islamic entity that embodies modern and anti-Islamic ideal is prevalent in TRMEs. Though, state sees TRMEs as 'backward' and an impediment to the advancement of society, the TRMEs regard state as an institution coming with all 'earthly innovations' so as to destabilize the equilibrium settled by the superstructure. Tribal order is a self-help system that sustains all necessary material and emotional needs by itself, and thus, it rarely requires the help of outsiders such as states. Nassim Jawad explains this phenomenon as follows:

> An Afghan Individual is surrounded… by concentric rings consisting of family, extended family, clan, tribe, confederacy, and a major cultural-linguistic group. The hierarchy of loyalties corresponds to these circles and becomes more intense as the circle gets smaller… seldom does an Afghan, regardless of cultural background, need the services and/or the facilities of the national government. Thus, in case of crisis, his recourse is to the kinship and, if necessary, the larger cultural group. National feelings and loyalties are filtered through the successive layers.[11]

Simply, it is the central government for the tribal order that occupies the periphery. TRMEs, traditionally, have seen little utility in the function of the central government. The conflict of the tribal order with the modern state generally arises in socio-economic issues such as land reform, whereby the state reallocates and redistributes the land with official deeds, and the allocation of water resources through large-scale irrigation projects. The land reform imposed by the states primarily threatens the territorial identity of the tribes. That is why the land reforms were to be the root causes of the *Basmachi* uprising in 1920-1925 in Central Asia against the Bolsheviks,[12] and the Kurdish uprisings in Southeastern Turkey in 1925-1930 against the newly founded Turkish Republic,[13] and the uprisings against the Abdulkarim Qasim Government in 1961 in Iraq.[14] The turmoil in rural Afghanistan under the Mohammad Sardar Daoud Khan (1973-1978) and Muhammad Najibullah Ahmadzai (1986-1992) rule[15] was the result of an ongoing debate in those states arising from unfinished land reforms in the rural areas, which aimed to establish absolute control of the lands by the state,

---

11 Nassim Jawad, *Afghanistan: A Nation of Minorities* (London, UK: Minority Rights Group International, Manchester Free Press, February 1992).
12 Rob Johnson, *Oil, Islam and Conflict* (London: Reaktion Books, 2007), p.20.
13 Metin Heper, *State and Kurds in Turkey* (New York: Palgrave Macmillan, 2008), p.189.
14 Charles Tripp, *A History of Iraq* (New York: Cambridge University Press, 2007), p.157.
15 Barnett R. Rubin, *The Fragmentation of Afghanistan* (London: Yale University Press, 2002), p.171.

distribution of the lands with the governmental deeds to the peasants, and tax extraction from the land and livestock.

Today, similar frictions between the state and tribes are rising in Iraq where the Iraqi government has initiated the Haweeja irrigation and land development project.[16] Similarly, Turkey has financed the Southeastern Anatolia Irrigation and Dam Construction Project,[17] which has mainly been hampered by the tribal order. Likewise, mainly due to the fierce resistance of local tribal leaders in rural Afghanistan the Najibullah government completely abandoned plans for social and economic transformation of the countryside, withdrew its military forces from the rural Afghanistan and ended the policies of disarming the tribes.[18] Ahmed Rashid observed the Afghanistan of 1989 as follows:

> In the countryside, Kabul is offering full local autonomy, any weapons up to and including tanks, as well as the money and titles to local leaders who can guarantee to keep open communications between the cities. The state controls the capital and few other towns, with tenuous negotiated control over the roads.[19]

Why then did the tribe emerge as the predominant organizational unit in pastoral life? Humans have been able to survive for centuries by gathering and organizing themselves as tribes against outside threats whether from; the other rival groups, wildlife, primitive living conditions or geographical challenges. Surrounded by many external threats, tribesmen and their families could only survive with the help of their tribe. The tribe has always been a support infrastructure in circumstances such as illness and the death of a family member. The members of the tribe are confident that they will never depart from their tribe, so they never feel isolation or loneliness. They know their enemies, their friends, and the roles they are expected to play in the tribe. Their identities in the tribe are respected, recognized and grounded. They enjoy the sense of belonging and significance. In addition, life is not complicated for them in this system since their utmost aim is to unquestioningly follow the footsteps of their ancestors. They also operate under the control of the tribal ethos, which consists of the set of norms created with the amalgamation of socialized Islam and traditional tribal code. This arranged lifestyle makes life in the TRMEs very simple, and does not require advanced educational skills. The code of honor requires that a tribe member upholds the tribe by showing bravery, fidelity,

---

16   Henry D. Astarjian, *The Struggle for Kirkuk* (Westport: Praeger Security International, 2007), p.14.
17   *Ntvmsnbc News Agency* <http://arsiv.ntvmsnbc.com/news/253255.asp> (accessed 13 July 2009).
18   Barnett R. Rubin, *The Fragmentation of Afghanistan* (London: Yale University Press, 2002), p.173.
19   Ahmed Rashid, 'Back to Feudalism', *Far Eastern Economic Review* (13 July 1989), pp.16-17.

hospitality, respect for elders and the families of other tribesmen, respect for the religious clerics and sacred places such as shrines and cemeteries, and hostility towards outsiders.[20]

Islam in TRMEs

The first thing that should be known about Islam in TRMEs is that there is no Islam *per se* that can be treated as a single, cohesive, coherent and monolithic entity. Like any other religion, Islam has been affected by major factors of life such as; economic class, access to the political power, ethnicity, gender, nationality, language, geography, local culture and history. To assume that the residents of TRMEs are driven to act exclusively by religion, apart from any other factor that shapes their lives is illogical.

What defines your way of life? What norms do you follow? If you ask these questions to any tribesman in TRMEs, the answer you would hear is that 'we live as our fathers devised. We are following tradition and we live as devout Muslims'. This ethos, which regulates the norms of tribal order, is two-fold: a mixture of *tradition* and *Islam* defining the way of life. The delicate equilibrium in the TRMEs is based on the amalgamation of a modified Islam, used to meet the tasks of regulating socio-economic life, and traditional tribal codes, *urf ad'at* or *tore*, which reflect the accumulation of highly revered regulative experiences. I will call the institutional mechanism that reflects the mixture of tradition and Islam and defines the way of life in TRMEs, as 'the superstructure'. It is this institutional mechanism, or the superstructure, that governed the TRMEs for centuries in a relatively peace and stable manner.

The amalgamation of a modified Islam, which is used to meet the tasks of regulating socio-economic life, with traditional tribal codes, which reflect the accumulation of highly revered regulative experiences are called ethics, or *akhlaq* in Arabic. Ethical modes of behavior, or *akhlaq*, in TRMEs are derived from either divine authority, or important religious figures, or pre-Islamic traditional codes. Since 'rights' and 'wrongs' are known because God tells us or tradition dictates in TRMEs, the basis for seeking the rights and wrongs through reasoning is severely discouraged. Put simply, authority not reasoning comes to the conclusion about correct action.

The ethical modes of behavior, or *akhlaq*, in the TRMEs must be defended from the outside world by the institutional mechanism, the fundamental principles of which control the people in the system. It is noteworthy that this superstructure is not Islam any more. Namely, there are many norms or established behaviors in the TRMEs despite being despised by Islam but upheld by the superstructure.

---

20 The movie '*Dances with Wolves*', directed and casted by Kevin Costner in 1990, successfully reflects these characteristics of a Native American tribe. In the same vein, the movie, '*The Last Samurai*', directed by Edward Zwick and casted by Tom Cruise in 2003, presents the rejuvenation of the soul of an American mercenary, who was lost and felt isolated mainly due to the side effects of the industrialized and materialized world, in a tribe in rural Japan.

For instance, bribe, though despised by Islam, is very prevalent in the TRMEs. This practice is legitimized and embraced by the superstructure as a type of recognized and ordinary social interaction.

Or, *kalum* money, given to the father of bride before the marriage in order to obtain sole rights to the bride's economic, sexual and reproductive services, is a tradition currently being practiced in many TRMEs in the world, though Islam severely discourages the implementation of it. Islam, in fact, which does not prescribe *kalum* money, encourages Muslims to give *mahr* money directly to the bride herself to ensure her immediate needs in case of a divorce. Islam prohibits fathers, brothers and husbands from taking *mahr* money given to the bride.

Or, the honor killings still prevalent in tribal order have been condemned many times by the Islamic scholars by issuing religious decrees.

Another example, which demonstrates the clash of Islam and tribal codes, is the tribal codes of Pashtuns in Afghanistan. Pashtuns are the largest and the most politically powerful ethnic group which adhere to the strict implementation of *Pashtunwali*, or doing Pashtu. The code of behavior stressing honor, or *namus*, is expressed by male Pashtuns through their ability to dominate and defend their property, including the household, wife and female relatives. A Pashtun who has suffered a blow to his honor is expected to seek revenge in the form of physical retaliation or compensation in property or money. Such a code of behavior is often in opposition to the tenets of Islam. When a conflict occurs, Pashtuns tend to 'do Pashtu' instead of following the *Sharia*.

Property, of course, is another example, which demonstrates the conflict of *Sharia*, the Islamic law, and tribal codes. According to the *Sharia*, the wife receives one-third of her husband's share, sons receive equal shares, and daughters receive half as much as a brother. For instance, this policy is rarely practiced in Afghanistan. According to the tribal codes practiced in rural Afghanistan, daughters receive nothing from their fathers. Widows receive nothing from their husbands as well and are, instead, cared for by their sons. The inheritance among brothers may also be unequal, that is, the oldest son usually inherits the name and political titles of his father along with the best land.

Nowruz, for instance, is a pre-Islamic Zoroastrian tradition dated back to the time of Achaemenids (648-330 BC). Although not being embraced by Islam, Nowruz, the very first day of the Spring, being a Zoroastrian holiday and having significance amongst the Zoroastrian ancestors of modern Iranians, is celebrated and observed as a Spring festival by the majority of the Muslim World, including parts of Central Asia, Afghanistan, Iraq, Turkey, South Asia, Northwestern China, the Crimea and some ethnic groups in Albania, Bosnia, Serbia and the Republic of Macedonia.

Another example of a pre-Islamic tradition currently practiced in some TRMEs is bound to the coming of the Spring and a pre-Islamic prophet named *Hızır* who has attained immortality by drinking the water of life, *ab-ı hayat*, and who has reached God. He is believed to wander around among people from time to time, especially in the Spring, and helps people in difficulty. *Hıdrellez Day* falls in the month of

May. Various ceremonies and rituals have been performed for various Gods with the arrival of Spring or Summer in Mesopotamia, Anatolia, Iran and in fact all Eastern Mediterranean countries since ancient times.

This collection of ethos is revered by everybody in the tribe and used by tribal leaders in their handling of intra-tribe relations since it meets every political, religious and socio-economic demand in the daily life of the tribal order. Moreover, the superstructure influences the system of inter-generational transmission of information. The younger generation receives only the information that promotes the preservation of the traditional way of life that regards the past as a *golden age*.[21] The sense of being attached to the past and the perpetual need of upholding and glorifying the past and the victorious ancestors is the key to the continuation of the tribal order in the TRMEs. For instance, among the Ghilzai tribe in Afghanistan, the sense of belonging to the tribe has Islamic underpinnings. That is, Ghilzais believe that they become Muslim at the time of Prophet Muhammad. Their ancestor named *Qays*, journeyed to Mecca and accepted Islam from Prophet Muhammad himself. Their long association with Islam not only provides a sense of 'seniority' for them among other ethnic groups but also amalgamate the tribal membership to the Muslim community, or *ummah*. Therefore, any Ghilzai feels his/her tribal solidarity as an Islamic one, and thus perceive anything that threatens tribal solidarity as evil and associated with the devil. I encountered several stories with the same references told by the members of the Barzan tribe, the ruling tribe in Northern Iraq.

These are supportive examples to prove the argument which suggests that the superstructure, which regulates the tribal order, is not equal to Islam. That is why labeling any phenomenon as *Islamic* in TRMEs would be an easy way to explain the phenomena, but not necessarily true all the time.

Different interpretations of the Islamic theology in TRMEs is another important aspect which contributes to my argument that Islamic radicalism, as a concept understood by any ordinary Westerner, is not the single root cause to address all contemporary dynamics in the TRMEs. There are various sources of Islamic theology and *Sharia*, or the system of Islamic jurisprudence. The *Quran* and the sayings of the Prophet *hadith* are the primary sources. Arguments about how the information in the *Quran* and *hadith* should be extended are based on the secondary sources; *qiyas* (reasoning by analogy) and *ijma* (scholarly consensus). Mainly because of the difficulty in deciding legal matters based on the *Quran* and *hadith*, many different interpretations of Islam came into existence over the course of time.

Religious succession is at base of *Sunni/Shia* differences. Over the course of the time, the *hadith* sayings of the Prophet formed the body of material from which one could extract the Prophet's ethical and religious model of exemplary behavior (*sunnah*). This Prophetic example, or *sunnah*, was so important that it became the basis of the

---

21 Sergei P. Poliakov, *Everyday Islam: Religion and Tradition in Rural Central Asia* (New York: M. E. Sharp, 1992), p.9.

name of the largest sectarian division in Islam, known as *Sunni* and claims to emulate the model of the Prophet. Over the course of time, the Islamic texts appeared, or *ilmihal*, in the Islamic literature as the sources of correct behavior, which standardized compilations of the *hadith* reports and the actions of the Prophet. In these texts, social and economic issues from daily routines such as; commerce, greetings and asking permissions, marriage, governing, justice, poverty, hunting, sacrifice, foods, clothing, medicine and divination, funerals and punishments, and psychological issues such as; dreams, patience, weeping, and fear took places in addition to the religious topics. *Abu Hanifa*, an Islamic scholar who lived in Iraq in 8th century, was one of the earliest legists and the founder of the *Hanafi* School in the *Sunni* world. This school achieved preeminence under the Abbasid Caliphate (750-945), spreading East from Iraq to Afghanistan and Central Asia. With the rise of the Ottomans, who favored this school as their official interpretation, the *Hanafi* School consolidated its position as the primary *Sunni* school. Currently, roughly 60 percent of world Muslims follows this school.[22] Since he separated 'belief' from 'practice' in Islam and accorded primacy to the belief, *Abu Hanifa*'s interpretation of *Sharia* was tolerant of differences within Muslim community.

Through time the *Shia* School has developed its own rituals and legal traditions, though they do not differ from *Sunnis* on the core issues regarding faith. All *Shia* acknowledge that Ali is the official successor of the Prophet and believe that the male descendants of Ali, or the *Imams*, are uniquely qualified to lead the Muslim community. Early theologians of the *Shia* School regarded the existence of prophets as a necessary outcome of God's mercy.[23] These scholars reasoned that the notion of mercy is one of divine attributes, and given the weakness and imperfection of human nature, it is impossible for humanity to overcome ignorance and suffering without the aid of divine knowledge. This divine knowledge is communicated by God to humanity through the chosen 'Imams' to deliver the message. While Muhammad is regarded as the last Prophet, the *Shia* scholars contend that the divine mercy continues after his death through the charismatic Imams. This concept of the *Shia* School has led to the primary area of conflict within the *Sunni* world, the succession of the Prophet's authority. In 680 BC, the murder of Imam Husayn – the son of Ali – by tyrannical Umayyad Caliph Yazidin in Karbala-Iraq, is considered as the most atrocious symbol of *Shia's* persecuted status in a largely *Sunni* world.

In the beginning of 9th century, specifically the Muslims from the tolerant *Hanafi* School started to fall away from the austere cult preached during the time of the Prophet and adopted practices that made it more *personal* and *emotional*. Geography and tradition also deeply accelerated this emerging 'diversification' in interpreting Islam. Whereas the tribal order requires a strict loyalty to the kin, only the traditional

---

22 Carl W. Ernst, *Following Muhammad: Rethinking Islam in the Contemporary World* (London: University of North Carolina Press, 2003), p.80.
23 Ibid, p.81.

Sufi[24] networks have been recognized as structures that are not defined with kinship in the tribal order. *Sufi* order, the sole alternative social network which prevails kin, tribal and ethnic affiliations, generally centers on the creation of a brotherhood that follows a leader, or *sheikh*, *pir* or *mayan*, who teaches a particular religious discipline to follow, or *tariqah* (way). The foundation of *Sufi* understanding is the covenant (*biat*) established between God and humanity at the beginning of creation. The *Quran* (7:12) says that: 'when your Lord brought out their offspring from the children of Adam, from their backs, and made them testify to themselves: 'Am I not your Lord?' They said, 'Yes, we have borne witness."

According to the teaching of the *Sufi* orders this was a sort of pre-eternal moment that the destinies of all humanity were sealed. Those who answer 'yes' would be obedient servants of God, and those who did not reply would be the rebels. This intimate primordial scene is, therefore, considered as an acknowledgement of divine authority, and for spirituality, as a testimony to the intimate relationship between God and humanity.[25] The theorizing point in *Sufi* teaching is the 'divine love of God', or simply, the understanding of 'God may be reached through love'.

According to the *Sufis*, God cherishes and sustains humans, while humanity recognizes this and agrees to submit to God's will. Since they seek for establishing a living intimacy between God and human soul through mystic methods, non-violent and apolitical *Sufi* networks, or *tariqahs*, they are inclined to refrain from intervening in the socio-political life of the society. It should be stressed that *Sufi* networks have no political agenda. *Tariqahs* such as *Naqshibendhi*[26] in Iraq and Turkey, and *Mawlawis/Qadiris* in Afghanistan have managed to create a sense of brotherhood in TRMEs regardless of their follower's tribal and ethnic affiliation. In traditional terms, *tariqahs* have functioned under the legacy of the central authorities or the tribal leaders as non-violent and pacifist social networks, which were responsible for non-profit tasks

---

24   The term 'Sufi' comes from the Arabic word of 'wool', which is the rough garment of ascetics, symbolizing self-denial.
25   Carl W. Ernst, *Following Muhammad: Rethinking Islam in the Contemporary World* (London: University of North Carolina Press, 2003), p.111.
26   This is the most prominent *Sufi* sect which is the predecessor of *Yasaviya* and aims to reach to Prophet Muhammad (PBH) with the spiritual lineage to the first Caliph Abu Bakr. Whereas the *Shia* school of Islam traces its lineage to Ali, the son-in-law of the Prophet, the founder of this sect, *Baha-ud-Din Naqshband Bukhari* (1318-1389) praised *Hulafa-i Rashidin* (Four Caliphates including Ali). This sect aims to reach the doctrine of oneness of Allah (Tawhid) through simplest, tolerant and easiest approaches. It does not demand from its followers strict and unquestionable obedience, and praises the real *Jihad* which would best be described as the inner struggle to improve oneself. According to the teaching of this sect, change is inevitable and Islam would be interpreted and reviewed over the course of the time and with the changing conditions in the society (*Ijtihad*-renovation). Unlike the Wahhabist or Pakistani Deobandis, which reject all forms of *ijtihad*, this sect approves the interpretations of *Mujeddidun*, the imams who aims to renovate, remodel and reform the pillars of Islam.

such as health care, housing, and providing basic services to the society without any political agenda. By managing tax-free *Waqfs*,[27] properties/lands donated by wealthy believers to support charitable activities and managed by social workers along with providing free social services, these *tariqahs* could finance themselves. The shrines of both *Shia* Imams and *Sufi* saints are also the centers of tremendous wealth and power coming from the visitors as wells as pious donations. These tomb-shrines, or the social magnets that entice people, have been institutionalizing certain kinds of entrenched authority by the local population. Thus, religious leaders of these networks managed to create enough room for the function of the networks inside TRMEs with the endorsement of the tribal leaders and the recognition of the people. But this socio-economic and political space created by the traditional Islamic networks in TRMEs has never been as powerful as the one created in the Christian world, which means that they have never attempted to assume the governance in TRMEs. More importantly, *Waqfs* run by these traditional Islamic networks have never resulted in fights for the political power. Instead, those who managed the *Waqfs* have typically gotten along with the executive power – the tribal order in TRMEs. The utmost aim of the *Sufi sheikhs*, who in general have a reputation as men of peace and seem disinterested in mundane political conflicts, is to preoccupy themselves and their followers with the individual's relationship to God. In the TRMEs where family, territory, property and power are of the utmost importance, *Sufi sheikhs* relinquishing these are viewed as both 'devout' and 'divine'. That is why they embrace the rule of obeying to the political ruler, or *ul'ul emr*, as the primary imperative in their teachings as long as it governs with justice. The *hadith* from *Abdallah Ibn Umar* has been one of the principles cited by *Sufis* to confirm this submissive characteristic of *Sufi* networks. *Abdallah Ibn Umar* said that 'The Messenger of God said that 'a Muslim has to listen to and obey (the order of his ruler) whether he likes it or not, as long as his orders involve not one in disobedience (to God), but if an act of disobedience (to God) is imposed one should not listen to it or obey it.'"[28]

Mullahs, another religious class in the TRMEs, however, interpret this *hadith* with focusing on the later part of it. *Mullahs* are paid religious teachers, who are supposed to be learned in the *Quran* and *Sharia*. *Mullahs*, who are not generally member of a traditional *Sufi* networks, are respected as the qualified arbiters of social disputes in the society as well as elementary school teachers. *Mullahs*, as spiritual leaders, play a crucial role in TRMEs because they are often the only literate person in the rural community where a great majority of whom cannot read. In contrast to the *Sufi sheikhs*, the *Mullahs*' role as religious arbiters forces them to take positions on religious issues,

---

27 Waqf are Islamic charity institutions which include mosque, hospital, school, bazaar and free meal house – the funding of which was facilitated by the donations of the rich people. Waqfs had been the center of gravity in societal, economic and cultural terms for centuries in Muslim countries.
28 Sahih Bukhari, *Hadith No. 203*, Vol. 4.

and these positions have political ramifications.[29] Any religious leader with a distinct political agenda would be called *Mullah* in TRMEs. *Mullahs* must also insist on their correctness of their stand in a particular issue to maintain their legitimacy before the folks they are in charge. That is why the proponents of the various positions often accuse those who disagree with them of being infidels, *kafir*, which is still a common practice in TRMEs. *Mullahs* are generally in opposition to *Sufi* networks by blaming that the function of these networks is opposed to the spirit of *Sharia*, which ideally stresses uniformity in Muslim behavior and addresses politics, economics, and family relations in addition to the religious practices. Even some hardline *Mullahs* condemn *Sufi* networks as apostasy by blaming that they disgrace the rules of *Sharia*. It also should be stressed that the *Mullah* class does not necessitate social stature to gain fame and fortune in rural Afghanistan, and thus, for a young man from a landless and disgraced family, to be a *Mullah* may be the sole option to change his destiny to join the 'elite club' through *Madrassa*.

Unfortunately, the utmost challenge in the TRMEs of many Muslim populated states such as Afghanistan, Iraq and Pakistan is that, a sizeable number of *Mullahs* embrace *Wahhabi/Salafi* interpretations of Islam stemming from strict *Hanbali School*.[30] *Wahhabi/Salafi* interpretation, the alternative version of Islam currently represented by puritanical Islamic movements such as al-Qaeda, is based on the teachings of Muhammad ibn Abd al-Wahhab (1703-1792), author of the *Kitab al Tawhid* (the book of monotheism). *Salafi understanding*[31] is considered as the major trend in contemporary fundamentalist movements, which is ideologically against change and adaption, and thus a closed and inflexible representative of Islamic jurisprudence. *Wahhabism* aims at purifying Islam from so-called *bid'a* innovations, or non-Islamic traditions and customs rooted from heresy, idolatry and other deviances. The principal aim of this interpretation is to practice Islam as the Prophet and his first disciples used to practice it to regain the last preeminence. According to them, this puritanical tradition, revealed by God himself and intended for all human race, is believed to be the sole acceptable form of Islam and all other unorthodox deviances are to be eliminated. For example, *Wahhabism* bans the cult of saints or the visit of holy tombs of saints, which are the integral part of religious practices in *Sufi* and *Shia* Islam. *Wahhabism*, specifically, is at odds with the *Shia* School since it rejects the hierarchical status of *Imams* in Islam, the backbone of *Shia* indoctrination. They even propose the erection of luxurious gravestones or mosques. Some of the most extreme *Wahhabi*sts even ban

---

29   Louis Dupree, *Afghanistan* (Oxford University Press, 2002), p.100.
30   Hanbalism, the alternative of Hanafism, is a theological and law school within the Sunni community developed by Ahmad ibn Hanbal. It considers that there are no other religious sources than the Quran and the Sunna (the Prophet's tradition, and thus, rejects the secondary sources, *ijma* and *qiyas*). The hanbalism, which is the most rigorist and purist school of Sunni Islam, is almost exclusively present in Saudi Arabia and Qatar.
31   As-salafi: used to indicate the Muslims who follows the teaching of the Prophet Muhammad and successors of the Prophet Muhammad.

gravestones, on which the names of the people and their family roots written, and minarets as recent inventions that encourage idolatry. According to this School, Islam is purely and inherently perfect. Any attempt to change or reformulate Islam, therefore, is an attempt to subvert God's will. The world is decadent, violent, unjust, aggressive and riddled with contradictions. In this light, Islam offers a powerful prescription. The proponents of this school surmise that increasing incursions of Western culture such as education, law, customs and values as being significantly more destructive in the long run because it directly threatens the core of the identity of Muslim community, or *ummah*. They also assert that the roots of the contemporary problems Islam faces with worldwide and the current backwardness of Muslim world is not because of lack of modernization, but primarily because of exogenous inputs coming with excessive modernization and Westernization.

This doctrine became very fashionable in the 1740s in Saudi Arabia when *Wahhab* found an ally, *Mohammad ibn Saud*, the founder of Saudi Arabia. Consequently, *Wahhabism* achieved a state-sponsored impetus and turned out to be official political ideology of Saudi Arabia and Gulf states after the marriage of state and the clergy.[32] It then spread to all provinces of the Kingdom/Gulf and drastically changed all indigenous religious practices in the Arabian Peninsula. *Wahhabism* played a great role in the initial political mobilization of Islamist groups in colonial India and Egypt. Hasan al-Banna of Egypt and the movement of Muslim Brotherhood in the 1930s, and Mawlana Maudoodi of Pakistan and the movement of *Jamaat-I Islami* in the 1940s, emerged as the prototypes for all later fundamentalist groups, where these figures and organizations employed the reformist rhetoric of claiming to return to the 'original' form of Islamic faith.[33] This strategy was also designed to discredit rival Islamic scholars and teachings, on the grounds that they represented corrupt deviations from the true path. For them, the solution to the crisis of Muslim communities in their respective regions lies in indoctrinating the people with socio-religious reforms while changing the governments with political reforms at the same time. Specifically, *Sayyid Qutp's* uncompromising de-legitimization of all 'man-made' political entities, including secular governments, has become the core of the *Salafi* movement. Islamists, therefore, vehemently criticize the elimination of God from the government and public space.[34] They believe that all domains in the life of Muslims should be ordered according to God's command, in this way it would be possible to eliminate the sins and weakness to which human decisions are prone. Islam, hence, has many premises for political and socio-economic issues. *Qutp* sees modern the Western-dominated world order as analogous to the pre-Islamic era of Arab paganism

---

32 *CRS Report for Congress*, 'The Islamic Traditions of Wahhabism and Salafiyah' (January 2008). Full report: <http://www.fas.org/sgp/crs/misc/RS21695.pdf> (accessed 24 October 2010).
33 Ibid.
34 Sayyid Qutp, *Milestones* (Kazi Publications, 2003), p.1.

– *Jahilliyah or ignorance* – against which the Prophet had struggled to re-establish the straight path, or obedience to God.[35] From this point of view, the first struggle should not be against the Western enemy as such but against the Westernizing enemies at home, who have imported and imposed infidel ways on the Muslim population. It should also be stressed that the dream of Islamic state is often more powerful when it remains vague and unspecified. Islam could be a remedy for any problem no matter in which realm this would be.[36] Islam would even solve social and economic injustices, corruption, unjust distribution of wealth and unemployment. The *Salafi/Wahhabi* School clearly addresses what to do to correct these problems, but gives no reliable roadmap how to do it. For instance, Osama bin Laden argued that al-Qaeda is the world's only hope for solving the global warming crisis.[37] According to bin Laden, talking about climate change was not an intellectual luxury, but an actual fact whose importance cannot be dismissed.[38] Similarly, Carl W. Ernst presents a highly relevant anecdote from prerevolutionary Iran to illustrate that how the appeal of Islam was presented by the Islamists as the universal solution that fits all problems in the society.

Tehran is a city that expanded far beyond its planned infrastructure, due to the migration of millions of people from rural areas. One of the results is that there is still a system of open sewers alongside the streets. During the last year of the Shah's reign, someone was overhead complaining bitterly about the sewers. 'Don't worry' replied the listener, 'that will be taken care of – by Islam'. Although the speaker had no specific connection in mind that would stretch from classical Islamic texts to the installation of a new sewer system, the remark illustrates that how the solution to all modern problems can be sought from Islam.[39]

This explicit example clearly proves that, with proper perception management techniques and appropriate messages, many Muslims who live in societies in which deprivation, social unjust and illiteracy prevail, could even believe that Islam will even solve the problem of open sewers alongside the streets. How to fix this problem? The *inshallah* (with God's help) concept will be best answer one would hear. That is why the *Wahhabi/Salafi* teaching, which proposes a divine-referenced governance model with global aspirations stands on the foundation of *decisive fear* and *vague promise*, perfectly fits for the immediate material needs and utopist ideas of many Muslims, who reside in corrupted, unjust and deprived TRMEs.

To achieve the objective of global supremacy in the Muslim World and Islamic purification, beginning in the 1960s, Islamists from around the world found safe harbor, employment and direct/indirect support in Saudi Arabia.[40] These included Osama

---

35   Ibid.
36   Ibid, pp.35-82.
37   Jarret Brachman, 'Watching Watchers', *Foreign Policy* (February 2010), pp.60-67.
38   Ibid.
39   Carl W. Ernst, *Following Muhammad: Rethinking Islam in the Contemporary World* (London: University of North Carolina Press, 2003), p.135.
40   *CRS Report for Congress*, 'The Islamic Traditions of Wahhabism and Salafiyah'.

bin Laden's teacher, the Palestinian preacher Abdullah Azzam, who was given the opportunity to establish educational organizations in Saudi Arabia and many Muslim states, which were soon to be hubs for the people suffering from the absence of free and qualified education in those states,[41] nurturing the environment of radicalism from which Osama bin Laden and his associates emerged.

In the early 1980s, the Saudis systemically began exporting *Wahhabism* across the globe, especially Pakistan, Afghanistan and Central Asia.[42] Azzam personally went to Pakistan with the support of the Muslim World League (MWL), a mighty Saudi-funded enterprise that was established as a charity organization. Azzam was aided by a branch of the MWL known as the International Islamic Relief Organization (IIRO), which played a key role of laying the foundation for the Afghan resistance against Soviet invasion.[43]

After the Soviet withdrawal from Afghanistan, the symbiotic relationship between the House of Saud and the *Wahhabi* clergy expanded and the royal family gave the latter more power and influence in order to strengthen its global front against *Shia* of Iran and moderate *Sunni* schools such as traditional *Sufi* networks. Also, oil money has exuberantly funded the export of radical *Wahhabism* and the terrorist activities executed by the latter. Oddly enough, because of global dependence on oil, the very sensitive global oil market and the money that came from the Gulf countries which uphold *Wahhabi* ideology, the international community, including the US, which is desperately dependent to the oil of Arabian Peninsula, would not be able take any concrete step against the rise of radical *Wahhabism*.[44] Thus, as it is postulated in the Counterterrorism Conference which was held in Riyadh in 2005, 'the world cannot defeat terrorism without Saudi Arabia defeating terrorism on its own grounds'.[45]

Unfortunately, very few people in the Muslim world can question the legitimacy of *Wahhabism*, practiced by the guardians of the holy cities of Islam, since it turned out to be the dominant part of undeniable national identity of the Arabian Peninsula in which the Prophet Muhammad and his fellow followers lived. The best answer to the question why the *Wahhabi* School of Islam attracts many non-Arab Muslims in the world, including the ones in TRMEs, is likely because it appears to be closest geographically, because of the holy cities, Mecca and Medina and linguistically in contrast to the Christianity, in which any Christian may worship in Aramaic, Greek,

---

41 *Center for Religious Freedom of Hudson Institute Report*, '2008: Saudi Arabia's Curriculum if Intolerance' (2008), Full report: <http://www.hudson.org/files/pdf_upload/saudi_textbooks_final.pdf> (accessed 21 January 2009).
42 *CRS Report for Congress*, 'The Islamic Traditions of Wahhabism and Salafiyah'.
43 Interview with Dore Gold, former Israeli ambassador to the UN <http://www.meforum.org/article/537 (21> (accessed January 2009).
44 David B. Ottoway, 'US Eyes Money Trails of Saudi-backed Charities', *Washington Post* (19 August 2004).
45 Rachel Bronson, 'Rethinking Religion; The Legacy of US-Saudi Relations', *The Washington Quarterly 28:4* (2005), p.121.

Latin, Hebrew, Arabic and even with his/her own language, Islam dictates the supremacy of Arabic as the original worshipping language. It is 'mandatory' in Islam to worship in Arabic, which means that to use one's native language is prohibited whilst worshipping, and to worship spiritually to the original faith practiced during the time of Prophet Muhammad. Moreover, due to the pilgrimage rule, or *haj* in Islam, millions of Muslim from all over the world visit Mecca and Medina, it is a practice which enables the *Wahhabi*sts to disseminate their indoctrination among world Muslims with no significant effort and amount of money. *Wahhabism*, therefore, entices many non-Arabs, who endeavor to purify themselves from the eroding effects of Westernization and modernization.

Let me tell an anecdote at this point. In the early 1990s, my villager uncle, who barely reads Turkish, went to Saudi Arabia to fulfill his pilgrimage obligation. In the early 2000s, a decade later, one of my friends who is fluent in Arabic and I, went to his house in the village. During our conversation, we started talking about his pilgrimage stories. He said that he had a question about a leaflet in Arabic of which he found when visiting the holy *Kaba*. He went to his bedroom and turned back with an attractive box. He opened the box very gently, and took a well wrapped package and said that 'I found this holy leaflet when encircling *Kaba* and I could not throw it to the trash since there are verses from *Quran* written on it. I, therefore, kept it for ten years in my house as a sacred object to bless my home'. My friend asked for his permission to inspect the leaflet. As soon as he looked it, he could not help from laughing. He said that 'uncle, the leaflet you kept ten years with care is a cook receipt of an Arabic magazine'. The grim fact in this funny anecdote is that to what extent the mentality in TRMEs is 'receptive' to anything Arabic. I cannot imagine how a mentality, which kept a cook receipt ten years with care by thinking that it is a part from holy *Quran*, would embrace the Arabs with the words of Islam in their mouths with open arms. It should be stressed then, that this receptiveness of TRMEs of anything Arabic endows a strategic superiority for the *Wahhabi*sts to disseminate their version of Islam in TRMEs.

It is also worth noting the importance of mosques in TRMEs, which are not simply places to pray but social hubs. Mosques are not places solely for worshipping; they instead provide a forum for socio-political interactions. It can also serve as a school, as a medical clinic, a housing facility for guests that visit the village, or a ceremonial place where important events are held. Thus, it is fair to state that the one who controls and runs the mosque in TRMEs controls the large part of the social life in that specific village/district. Anybody who sees the mosque simply as a worshipping place and disregards its mission as a socio-political hub in TRMEs makes a strategic mistake. The question of who currently controls mosques in rural Afghanistan and exploiting Friday prayer sermons to disseminate its rhetoric is a highly important – though neglected – question directly linked to the end state of the COIN in Afghanistan. Therefore, to apply the famous motto in modern COIN doctrine, *Clear-Hold-Build* to the mosques in TRMEs it carries utmost importance. Clearing the mosques from extremist ideas and individuals, supporting moderate and educated

Imams, strengthening the mosques as socio-political magnets for the people would be the steps of this strategy. Supporting schools, health clinics and social halls around mosques would also be a good strategy in a state's effort to control the TRMEs.

In conclusion, Islam in any TRME may be defined as a 'modified' one that includes traditional tribal customs, teachings of *Sufi* orders and the doctrines of *Mullahs*. These three components interweave the superstructure; an institutional mechanism of meaning and social structure encompassing personnel practice, ideology and meaning. The multifaceted 'modified Islam' is rich in meanings and plays multiple roles in the society. Modified Islam looms as the most significant 'commonality' in highly diversified rural Afghanistan and; lends meanings to the lives of individuals, comforts and channels the ire of the deprived, forms a medium for political coalitions, is inseparable for some tribal identity, functions as the constitution of rural areas, and lastly is included in all Muslim Afghan's most basic identity. Put simply, the tribal leaders at the execution seat, the *Sufi sheikhs* and *Mullahs* at the judiciary and legislation, who are fully aware of the rights and responsibilities of other constituent players, have formed a delicate equilibrium when governing TRMEs for centuries. A check and balance system, therefore, could be established and a healthy way of the distribution of power could be facilitated with this triple system.

Tribes and Politics

In political terms, the inter-tribal world could be described by the term 'anarchy'. As states in the current international system, tribes are quasi-autonomous and self-help entities which aim to maximize their relative power in the anarchic order. It is not an exaggeration to assert that all tribal leaders should be offensive realists by nature to survive in the system. Tribes have two primary political objectives in the tribal order. The first objective is to establish a balance of power among the tribes by building tribal confederations, and allying with other tribes to fend off hostile tribes. Second, when a central authority emerges, the tribal order, first, tries to avoid any disagreement with it, and then seeks to keep the central authority engaged by helping to create an alternative political force against the government so as to survive. The example of the Taliban, as an alternative political movement disregarding the central government, would serve perfectly as a means for the tribal order to keep the government engaged. The tribal order should exploit both of them to survive. These objectives explain why tribes are very dynamic and apt to change and adapt to the ever-changing political environment. They may establish temporary alliances, or modify their alliances overnight, since political allegiances of the tribes are in a permanent state of flux. Battles between tribes are never fought so fierce that one side attempts to annihilate the other completely. Rather, when it is apparent that one side is winning, the other side temporarily retreats and immediately looks for other tribes to align with. More importantly, tribes may change sides in battle when the other side is winning. A common perception is that the other side is winning because it is God's will and one should not oppose God's will. In the light of the current developments in Afghanistan, this is certainly the case at the moment.

Temporary truces and alliances are common. Loyalty can be rented, but the term length of the rental is uncertain. Disparate tribes are almost never able to completely unite around any specific political issue except for maintaining their autonomy.

In Afghanistan, there are some tribes that pretend to support the Coalition Forces which try to market central government, there are tribes which look natural, and some others which pretend to support the Taliban. All tribes in rural Afghanistan constantly have to change sides in accordance with the changing political dynamics in order to survive. Tribes, therefore, have always been both a part of a solution and a part of a problem for the central governments. Similarly, there were three categories of Kurdish tribes in Northern Iraq based on to their political preferences: those which support Baghdad, those that remain neutral, and those that support a rebellion against the central government during the 1990s. Thus far, it has proven impossible for Baghdad to suppress uprisings without allying with the pro-Baghdad Kurdish tribes (*Jash*) or trying to gain the support of the neutral tribes.[46]

For instance, Husayn Surchi, the leader of pro-Baghdad Kurdish *Surchi* tribe during the famous Anfal Campaign of the Iraqi Security Forces in 1988, told rebellious tribes that 'my villages are still standing and are still wealthy, my people still dress as Kurds, speak Kurdish and have a good life. Look what your nationalism has done for you. Your villages are destroyed, your people have been forcibly re-settled, you live in exile and you have nothing left. Why call me a traitor?'[47] This same tribe ended up switching sides with an overnight political decision in December 1994 during the bloody five-year long intra-Kurdish civil war. The villages of this tribe were to be wiped out by the forces of the Kurdish Democrat Party (KDP), a traditional tribal confederation led by Massud Barzani since the *Surchi* tribe allied itself with the Patriotic Union of Kurdistan (PUK) for territorial benefits.[48]

Similarly, in Turkey, the Marxist-Leninist[49] Kurdish Workers Party (PKK) attacked wealthy tribal leaders and claimed that they were the representatives of the tribal system, which exploited the Kurdish peasants in Southern Turkey. The assassination of M. Bucak, a well-known conservative Kurdish politician and a wealthy tribal leader in Eastern Turkey, in 1979,[50] triggered still ongoing fights between the

---

46 Amatzia Baram, 'The Iraqi tribes and the Post-Saddam System', *Brooking Institution: Saban Center Report* (8 July 2003). Full text: <http://www.brookings.edu/papers/2003/0708iraq_baram.aspx> (accessed 29 June 2009).
47 David McDowall, *A Modern History of the Kurds* (New York: St. Martin's Press, 1996), p.377.
48 McDowall, *A Modern History*, p.16.
49 PKK has been recognized as a terrorist organization by the Department of State of the US and the European Union: <http://www.state.gov/s/ct/rls/other/des/123085.htm> and <http://eur-ex.europa.eu/LexUriServ/LexUriServ.do?uri=OJ:L:2009:023:0037:0042:EN:PDF> (accessed 13 June 2009).
50 Ali Nihat Ozcan, 'PKK Party Congress Sets Long-Term Strategy Based on Threat Perceptions', *Terrorism Monitor*, Volume 6, Issue 2, (2008): <http://www.jamestown.org/single/?no_cache=1&tx_ttnews%5Btt_news%5D=5234>

pro-state tribes and the PKK. On 18 October 2008, the PKK claimed responsibility for a violent attack in which 12 Kurdish villagers were killed in Southeastern Turkey. The confessions of a PKK terrorist captured after the attack, provides significant information about the impacts of tribal rivalry on the terrorism. The captured terrorist confessed that his group killed those villagers who were members of the pro-state Babat and Jirki tribes, mainly due to the local territorial disputes between the tribes in the region. He also stated that their commander, a member of the pro-PKK tribe in the region, ordered the execution of villagers from hostile tribes in order to terrorize the other tribes.[51]

In short, the tribal order is capable of exploiting any political issue between the central authority and the rival organizations that challenge tribal interest on any political issue between the rival tribal confederations. Likewise, for the central authority, it is difficult to eliminate the tribal order not only because of geographical and economic limitations of state authority, but also due to the triple political role (ally-neutral-enemy) played by the tribes. Furthermore, the standing of tribes collapses when the central government is principally strong both in military and financial terms, and this was evident during the reign of Amir Abdul Rahman Khan (1880-1901) in Afghanistan.[52] Tribal order also seem to be opportunistic in terms of its cooperation with the government depending on prospects for financial reward; that is, there is no unanimity in tribal interests except 'to maintain their autonomy'.

It is also noteworthy that the state borders are usually meaningless for tribes. Many tribesmen seasonally cross the borders with their flocks. More importantly, the tribes which live in the frontiers of the states, use the borders for smuggling as an important source of income. Likewise, permeable frontiers have offered sanctuary to the tribes by allowing them to cross to neighboring states. It is a common practice for a tribesman who committed a crime in state A to escape to his relatives living in state B by using traditional routes other than border gates. The current problem in the Afghanistan-Pakistan border and the ongoing interactions of the members of the same tribe yet the citizens of different states explicitly lays out this dilemma. Moreover, the construction of any political division within a state while ignoring the tribal realities would also threaten the internal stability and security of that specific state.

---

51 Details of the news from a prominent Turkish Journalist, Saygi Ozturk: <http://www.anahaber.com/haber-quotKatliami-kameraya-aldikquot-48510.html> (accessed 29 June 2009).
52 Roohullah Rahimi, 'Afghanistan: Exploring the Dynamics of Sociopolitical Strife and Persistency of Insurgency' (Pearson Peacekeeping Centre, Ottawa: Occasional Paper 2, 2008). Full report: <http://www.peaceoperations.org/wp-content/uploads/2010/02/OP2_Rahimi.pdf>

Social Hierarchy in TRMEs

In the order of priority, social hierarchy in the TRMEs is represented by; tribal leaders, religious leaders, village/neighborhood (*mahalla*) leaders, house/family leaders, adult and married males in the house in the priority of their ages, the most senior female in the house (the mother or the first wife of the house/family leader), bachelor males, unmarried females, the brides of the house, and lastly the children in the house.

The utmost aim of any tribal leader is to *survive*, not the implementation of *Jihad*. A perfect profile of the tribal leader constitutes charismatic and pragmatic leadership, a benign attitude toward his followers, loyalty to the superstructure, and well-honed intuition in regards to the changing inter-tribe political dynamics.

Village leaders in rural areas (*mukhtar*) or neighborhood leaders in the districts (*mahallas*) are the representatives of their villages/districts. They could either be assigned by the tribal leaders or elected by the people. Typically, elders in the community have the recognized authority to conduct any negotiations with the tribal leader or the outside world concerning any specific issue which interests that village/district. These intermediaries, to a certain extent, are the first and foremost political figures in the tribal order since they have to keep the delicate balance of the interest between the people in the village/district they live and the tribal leader.

Family

The basic unit of production in the tribal order is the household. The family both would be an extended family (a multigenerational family unit) or a fraternal joint family (two or more brothers with their views and children), but rarely a nuclear family. The house/family leaders are in charge of their families in the village/district and are regarded as the manager of the family affairs. They tend to avoid for as long as possible letting their sons, even if they are married and have children, leave the house, since the population in the house is the primary force behind the family leader. If he does not have enough manpower, that is to say in a small family, this not only means the absence of the workforce in the pastoral life, but also means being suppressed and politically demeaned by the other houses. More importantly, the excessive population in the houses means illiteracy and poverty in the village/district, which in turn contributes to the continuation of the tribal order.

In tribal order kinship descent is traced through males, and almost all property is inherited through men. As property is passed patrilineality, so are the feuds about previous inheritance. Relations with maternal kin tend to be marked by cordiality and helpfulness, since maternal relatives are not competitors in the political and economic areas. The Arab proverb commonly used in Iraq, 'I against my brother, my brother and I against my cousin, my cousin and my brother and I against the world', is a good example to address the problems in the paternal linkages. Or an Afghan proverb, 'do you have an enemy? I have a cousin', clearly frames the fact as to what extent paternal relations would be problematic.

Uprising is a common phenomenon in the house. It is not easy for any member of the family to raise an issue that would challenge the authority and power of the father, even if he or she raises the issue through negotiations and compromise. For instance, the decision of a married son to leave the house is highly sensitive. It can easily give way to a rivalry between authoritarian father and a rebellious son. Because of the likelihood that neither side is open to compromise, conflicts between father and son often result in the permanent alienation of the son and his family from the house, and can even lead to violence.

Life in a multi-wife half-sibling environment under one roof of a typical house in a TRME creates interesting challenges, which might be difficult to understand for a Western mindset. First, although the father controls the external affairs of the house, his authority inside the house is typically weak. Meanwhile, the relationship between the mother and the eldest son is usually special, and the eldest son is like a father figure for his brothers and sisters. Any issue related to the mother and her children is typically handled by the mother and the eldest son in a discreet manner that does not involve the rival wives or half-siblings. This is so that the rival wives do not use these issues to erode the position of the wife and her children.

Meanwhile, the rivalry between the first wife and the second typically has important consequences, as both vie for control of the internal affairs in the house. I personally witnessed this interesting phenomenon in Iraq during my interview with a village leader who stated that his first wife would only let him to marry again with his second wife on the condition that she would select the third wife by herself. The aim of the first wife was surely to isolate the second wife in the house by permanently controlling the third one. We may conclude then, that even in the house, there is a political rivalry amongst the wives to control the internal affairs in the house. If this is the house of the tribal leader or village/district leaders, the first wife (*hatun*) is the most prominent political advisor to the tribal or village leader, having an important role in the shaping of the tribe's political decisions. It is likely to assert that, in the Western world, the standard picture of Muslim women who are oppressed by men, restricted to the home, and veiled in public is not always true in TRMEs. The old saying of 'the whisperings of the first wife to the ear of her husband look like the lullabies of his mother' has been widely cited to emphasize the power of the first wife. In contrast to arguments which contend that women in highly paternalistic TRMEs are harshly suppressed, this point suggests that the absence of women in the streets or café houses does not mean that all women are slighted in TRMEs. Although the humiliation, harassment, and even honor killings of young women can be prevalent in this system, the authority of the senior lady, first wife or mother, over her husband/son – even if he was a tribal leader – is absolute. An anecdote from the city of Amediyah in Northern Iraq may elucidate this phenomenon. There had been a very cruel tribal feud rooted from the land dispute between Tirvanish and Zebar tribes in this ancient city. In this three decade-long dispute, more than a dozen males had been killed from both sides. During my service in this city in 1999, this feud continued and we heard that the efforts of reconciliation attempted by the major of the city, the ministers from Baghdad and even famous religious figures in the region were futile. The tribes incessantly refused any peace effort from these high profile figures. Two years later, when I returned back to the city in 2001, I learned that the feud was settled. It was shocking news for me since I had listened to many grim stories about this feud. I asked our interpreter to figure out how this feud was settled. He explained to me that in a Friday prayer, a senior lady from the Tirvanish tribe, who had recently lost her second son in this bloody conflict, went to the main mosque of the city and insulted the tribal leaders of both tribes before everybody by throwing her veil to the ground and making her hair seen. This was a practice so that the senior lady could humiliate the leaders of both tribes, who maintained this feud meaninglessly, before everybody. The tribal leaders then came to realize to what extent their stubborn motives had done to maintain the feud and impair the social life in their tribes, so they settled the dispute at that time. This anecdote clearly demonstrates the role of senior ladies in the system and their political power to settle things, if/when necessary.

The most viable option for a wife to challenge the authority of the first wife in the system and obtain the absolute control of the household as well as influence over her husband, is to give birth to as many sons as possible. She may obtain greater influence if she has more sons than the first wife. This tactic has resulted in excessive fertility and over population in the tribal order. For as much as is said about the dominance of the male in a TRME, it is actually the man's mother first – then the first wife (or the wife with the most sons) who holds the greatest influence in TRMEs. It would be a fatal mistake to underestimate the political power and absolute authority of the first wife over the control of the internal affairs in the house and over the decisions of her husband and her sons. Interestingly, the political decisions of the mother and first wife can have violent, even deadly implications on daughters that dishonor the family, tribe and the superstructure.[53] It is worth noting that since the women in TRMEs live in extended families and in acquainted communities, they could frequently access women's social networks, a fact which can be hard to find in the more atomized Western societies. As a childhood remembrance, the regular weekly meetings of all women in my village were a sort of joy for me since I could eat all the desserts I wanted with no limitations. I also remembered that how the women were crazy about listening to the gossips of some particular ladies, or 'the newspapers on foot' my mother called, on up-to-date news concerning our village. I, therefore, assert always that ladies hear first in TRMEs.

Collective Mentality in TRMEs

The TRME promotes a collective mentality. Any individual outside the protection of the tribe has to face the challenges of the rural lifestyle individually. Given the

---

53 The internal affairs in a TRME household has rarely been studied, mainly due to difficulties of access.

environment, this burden is almost impossible to face. Traditional Islamic networks also promote the collective mentality that causes their members to surrender to the sect, and never to selfishly pursue individual interests. This sense of selflessness, serving the good of the community, results in a readiness to give one's individual life for the sake of the common good of the TRMEs. Even if the tribesman dies, he knows his ultimate sacrifice would be for the benefit of the community. More importantly, given the threat of death for the collective good, he can be confident that his family will be cared for after his death. It is a lifetime commitment for a tribe to take care of the family of a fallen member, no matter the reason for his death. His wife would either re-marry someone in the tribe, preferably the brother of the deceased tribesman, or would remain a proud widow in the tribe. His boys would be matched with the children of their uncle as blood brothers and his daughters would be promised a cradle arrangement marriage. The peace of mind that this system inspires makes the tribesman more eager to fight for the collective cause of the tribe.

As an example, during a campaign in rural Iraq, the local tribal militia among whom the author was serving as a liaison officer were ambushed and four of them were killed by the insurgents. The author asked for a medical helicopter to evacuate the dead. Due to the Improvised Explosive Device (IED) threats in the theater, the pilot of the helicopter asked for an electronic search for IEDs in the prospective landing zone. Since there was no mine detector available, a local militia member who understood the situation jumped to the prospective landing zone and started to run around. While everybody in the group was lying down in the event of an IED explosion, the local militia member shouted that he was the detector and began jumping randomly in the landing zone. After roughly five minutes, the militiaman yelled that his mine search had been done and the helicopter could land safely. After the helicopter landed and the bodies were evacuated, the author asked the militiaman why he had behaved like this. The local militiaman answered:

> Sir, when I jumped into the landing zone, I was fully aware that I had two options, either to die or to survive. If there had been an IED in the landing zone and had me blown up, I knew that my tribe would deliver a small amount of land to cultivate for my family. Since my father is a landless and poor peasant, he would be happy for this and surely would take care of my wife and children for the rest of his life. They would all pray for me, which makes me happy. Because I survived, all the members of the militia, including my commander, will think that I am a hero, who risked my life for my fallen comrades. They would report me to the tribal leader and he would promote me. You see, either dying in that landing zone or surviving is gain for me. It is a win-win solution.

He also concluded his remarks by stating that 'the ones who think about their end cannot be heroes'. How would one analyze the decision-making process of this militia member from the perspective of a rational actor model? Without knowing his rationale for the behavior, one might conclude that he is totally out of his mind or is ignorantly brave. But knowing his rational, it was clear that he used a well-calculated and rational calculus in which the two alternative outcomes both lead to 'win' solutions.

Fatalism in TRMEs

> *Some lucky ones are born rich and with many privileges. I could not choose the place of my birth, my parents, or my physical and mental characteristics. As a poor villager, I was born in desperation and deprivation. I come to conclude that the only opportunity for me for self-actualization in this life is to decide time and manner of my death. May God bless me an honorable death.*
>
> A remark from a tribesman from the Barzan Tribe in Northern Iraq

Fatalism may be defined as a doctrine emphasizing the attaching of all events or actions to fate or inevitable predetermination. Since free will is highly discouraged in any TRME, 'acceptance' is an appropriate norm, rather than resistance against inevitability. The underlying factor in the prevalence of the concept of fatalism in TRMEs is not Islam, it is in fact, rural way of life that is shaped by; harsh terrain features, extreme climatic conditions, protracted draughts, prolonged famines and successive invasions. To cope with the difficulties coming with the rural way of life, showing diversity, ingeniousness and flexibility is not always enough. A fatalistic mentality, which indicates a higher level of belief that heavenly forces control life's outcomes and assures that, in the end, it's all up to God, is also an important factor to explain the tenacity and determination of the people in TRMEs.

In Islam, the concept of predestination, or *qadar*, postulates that the events of the world take place within God's knowledge and will. The *qadar* concept assumes that God has calculated out the span of every person's life, their lot of good or ill fortune, and the fruits of their efforts. God is omnipotent to intervene, quite inexplicably and suddenly, whenever He wants. That is why, when referring to the future, Muslims commonly qualify any predictions with the phrase *Inshallah*, or 'if God willed'. In TRMEs, God knows whether this year's harvest will be good or bad, God knows if the livestock could get through the disease, and in short, God knows best about every aspect of the environment that surrounds people. Specifically, the explanatory power of the concept of *qadar* is unprecedented when it comes to any issue with respect to life and death. God bestows a child or takes him/her back if He wants – that is why any policy of family planning is disgraced among people in TRMEs. God knows how, when and why to assess people with the death/killing of beloved family members or friends. By God's will, a tribesman saves his own life, or becomes a martyr. Any issue about the life and death is directly bound to the grand design of God, rather than being a coincidental one. Interestingly, the tribesman from Northern Iraq, whose remarks stated above, was not a devout Muslim he was instead, the one who embraced a secular way of life. This example indicates that the *qadar* concept of Islam is facilitated by everybody, whether being a devout believer or not, in TRMEs to justify and rationalize all actions. The fatalistic mentality has, therefore, turned out to be a sort of societal norm, not a religious one, which is embraced by everybody in TRMEs.

Justice in TRMEs

Some commodities were brought before Imam Ali and people came to take their share. In order that people should maintain discipline he kept the people at a distance by means of ropes and he, himself, distributed the whole of it to the representatives of various tribes. Afterwards, he found a piece of bread that was left in a container. He then ordered it to be divided into seven equal parts and like the other property gave one piece to each of the tribes.[54]

The notion of 'freedom' is the primary value associated with Western civilization when defining the relation between the individual and the governing political entity or the state. It is the notion of 'justice' the primary value associated with TRMEs that can only give enough legitimacy to govern in the people's eyes, particularly if they have experienced a serious breakdown of order. Justice is 'glue' that binds all features of any TRME and orders the society. Put simply, it is much more important to be 'justly' treated than to be 'secured' for the residents of TRMEs.

Firstly, the concept of social justice may be addressed in this section. Justice in Islam is termed *adl*, which in fact, literally mean to divide two things 'equally' or to maintain 'the balance'. Justice, or *adalat* in Arabic, is defined in TRMEs therefore, as equitable distribution of common goods and honors, consisting security, property and even social standing. The concept of *adalat*, which was used 104 times in the *Quran*, does not constitute an individualistic phenomenon which implies the need of Islamic society because of their need for one another, but rather, this 'communal' concept implies that the Muslims are obliged to look after one another, and more importantly to be the responsible for the preservation of the good of all. Since the *Quran* postulates that human beings are created weak,[55] it emphasizes on the *ummah* (community) solidarity not on individual's strength. The principles of *adalat*, is therefore, to provide a framework to assign rights and duties in the basic institutions of the society and define an appropriate distribution of the benefits and the burdens of social cooperation.

The Islamic principle of property suggests that the needy people have a right in the wealth of a rich person because everything belongs to God. Islam encourages the believers to spend in charity in different forms. In TRMEs, moral codes of behavior, or *akhlaq*, dictate that the right to private property has less importance than the duty to ensure social justice. In the traditional sense, the social responsibilities of wealthy believers relate to the dictum of the social support system, or *takaful* (mutual guarantee and solidarity) in four areas of cooperation: with the family, within the community, among communities, and through giving and endowments. With implementing

---

54 *Bihar-ul Anwar*, Vol. XLI, p.136.
55 *Holy Quran*, 'Woman – *Nisa* Section', 4:24.

takaful, wealthy believers in TRMEs seek to ensure equitable distribution of wealth in a community. Obligatory charity of wealth, or *zakat*, for instance, is the most important aspect of *takaful*. Muslims are supposed to pay 2.5 percent of their savings or income as *zakat* annually. The *Quran* provides specific guidelines in the distribution of *zakat* to the poor and needy. Thus, in the traditional sense, the doctrine of *zakat* would be regarded as the first system of social security in TRMEs.

Furthermore, with regard to justice, the Western mindset puts *accuracy* above all other considerations. In the Western world, a methodical and long process to find justice is always appropriate, since the environment provided by the authority of the state is secure enough to await a verdict. The Western mindset demands the decision of the judge to be accurate and objective. In contrast, people in TRMEs seek the swift implementation of justice rather than concern themselves with accuracy, since they do not have enough time and patience to wait. First, a TRME is an inappropriate setting for a prolonged legal dispute since there is no a superior authority to make both sides wait patiently and peacefully for the decision. Second, the uncertain result of any legal issue can cause more destructive consequences in TRMEs than the issue itself, potentially turning a crime into a tribal or inter-family feud, which could last for decades and claim the lives of many adult males. Thus, to reach a decision as soon as possible, which would somewhat satisfy each side and avoid inter-tribe or inter-family conflicts is preferable to a lengthy justice process.

That is why retaliation, *badal* or *kisas* or *hudud*, one of the basic principles of Islamic *Sharia* Law which justifies the proportionate use of violence in response to crime, is commonly used to implement justice. Retaliation also serves as a swift implementation of justice. It is noteworthy that the retaliation system is a perfect match for TRMEs since it is not only valid for everybody in TRMEs, including its wealthy and powerful members, but also limits the probability of corruption of justice because of its simplicity. Retaliation for wrongdoing is allowed, but the wronged person cannot do more harm than that received (equality), and it is better still to have patience and forgive. In addition, if the crime was involuntary or accidental, or the family of a guilty party would ask for pardon, an offer of *blood money* can settle the case. Interestingly, in some cases the victim's family may even forgive the offender if it is believed that the latter was right in his actions and the victim deserved this outcome. One should note that the retaliation rule is one of the causes of irrelevancy of the central government in TRMEs. That is, the retaliation rule, which is perfectly applicable to the individual punishment, is ineffective for the punishment of the crimes resulted from the government's policies and programs failures, which then require a fundamental overhaul of the legal system in TRMEs. Being a collective political entity, not an individual, the central government cannot be imported to the traditional legal system of TRMEs.

During a campaign in Iraq, Sheikh Ali, not only a tribal leader but also a descendant (*sayyid*) of the Prophet Muhammad, was in charge of the local militias that the author accompanied as a liaison officer. Besides enjoying two distinguished roles, being a tribal leader and a religious figure, Sheikh Ali also was a charismatic figure, who had full command of his militia. On the first night of an operation involving the infiltration to a target area, the tribe's militia rested whilst hiding in a jungle area. Whilst the liaison team was with Sheikh Ali, they heard a single shot from the area where the militia were resting. After a short period of confusion, everybody in the group came to conclude that something was terribly wrong since nobody heard other gun shots. Soon afterwards, some of the militiamen threw a beaten man in front of Sheikh Ali, who asked them to explain what was going on.

They explained that two militiamen, from different tribes but in the same unit, quarreled over a tomato. Initially, they had two tomatoes. When one man gave the other the smaller tomato, he refused to take it, and demanded the bigger one. Eventually, the quarrel over the tomatoes ended with the shot that killed one of the two. Sheikh Ali listened to the explanation silently. The killer was trembling in fear and despair on his knees. All of a sudden, Sheikh Ali grabbed his pistol, and shot two times to the chest of the murderer in front of everybody. Then he loudly announced that the operation was canceled and that the group had to turn back. He then turned to the liaison team headed by the author as if nothing special had happened and apologized very politely for the things they witnessed. More importantly, he also explained that if he had not solved the problem with this swift implementation of justice, the murder would have caused a tribal feud between the two tribes of the men involved and would result in many more deaths on both sides. Thus, the swift killing of the offender, justified by the retaliation, *kisas* or *badal* rule, was the most appropriate solution for the families of the two militiamen since there would not be an ensuing tribal feud.

One of the most important aspects of the Islamic principle of Justice in TRMEs is adherence to the law and order. The ruler then cannot make up new laws or ignore the basic principles of the moral codes of behavior. It also worth noting that, since the majority of population can neither read nor write and in TRMEs, the use of written texts of all sorts in all socio-political and economic interactions is relatively low. People do credit the words and oaths of others instead of written contracts. This concept of accountability through oral communications, which indicates how essential it is to be just to everybody, have constituted a prime necessity for everybody in TRMEs for centuries. This phenomenon also explains the prevalence of all kinds of oaths and swearing in the culture of TRMEs. 'God be witness, 'I offer you the name of God to fulfill this agreement', 'I swear to God that', 'I swear to my grandfathers that', and 'I swear to the honor of my family that', are the kinds of oaths you may hear in the local markets in TRMEs, which are used by the traders to conduct economic interactions. Similarly, in the local legal practices of TRMEs, oaths are attributed much greater weight than written evidence. Rather than being used simply to guarantee the truth of the testimony, they themselves are used in local legal practices as evidence. To be 'the person of his/her words' is thus, the utmost objective of all people in TRMEs so as to maintain their legacy of accountability.

Lastly, the people in TRMEs are inclined to believe that the concept of justice has been revealed by God. For them, this concept, that governs all sorts of human affairs, is only one facet of the universal set of laws settled by God, practiced by the forefathers for centuries and governed the TRMEs. Violation of this concept is therefore, not only a simple crime of the guilty ones, but also a big offense, or sin, against God. Put simply, the crime that violates the concept of justice is considered a sin as well, which the violator must ultimately answer to God on the Day of Judgment.

Violence in TRMEs

'Traditionally, feuds are caused by *zan* (women), *zar* (literally gold, symbolizing the portable property), and *zamin* (land or other immovable properties)'. This is a proverb commonly used by Afghan males and clearly indicates the causes of feuds in the tribal order.[56]

From the first glance, it would seem that the people in TRMEs feel that violence is the sole means to solve every problem in this system. In fact, as long as everyone abides by the tribal ethos and the tribal order, TRMEs are safe places. The tribal order provides a collective security umbrella for each individual in the system. Since any individual feels the power of the tribe behind his or her back, he or she can travel safely, conduct daily routines at home or the in the fields, and establish social contacts with other individuals with that collective security net to support him or her. Likewise, the occurrences of some types of crime such as theft are very rare in TRMEs since everybody knows each other.

However, the killing of adult males, as a punishment for violating tribal order, is common. Regardless of whether the men involved are in same tribe, issues such as; land dispute, disputes over water allocation, or disputes over grazing lands can result in killing. Assassinations in daytime ambushes are preferred since the killer then honorably claims that by conducting this assassination, he is on the right side of the dispute and has nothing to hide. Furthermore, since manly warrior pride is highly revered in TRMEs, any issue in the attack that raises questions regarding the attacker's honor and labels him *coward or shamed*, should be avoided at all costs. Thus, everybody in TRMEs not only knows who used violence and for what purposes but also grades the honor of the executer by the manner of the killing or attack.

For instance, during an operation in Iraq, the local militia and the author conducted an ambush near a village after receiving intelligence regarding a planned visit of insurgents to the village for supplies. Roughly two hours after positioning the ambush, three insurgents appeared. They stopped to take a break in the gardens just outside the village, in an area that happened to be 300 meters away from the ambush. The author proposed an immediate attack to the leader of the militia, but the militia leader gently declined the proposal claiming that 'to attack from secret posts when the enemy is on their property is dishonorable to them. Hence, it would be better to wait for the enemy to leave from their property and then conduct the attack'.

Since any tribal dispute can turn into a tribal or inter-family feud that can last for decades and takes the lives of dozens of adult males, the retaliation rule of the *Sharia*

---

56 Louis Dupree, *Afghanistan* (Oxford University Press, 2002), p.127.

Law can be applied in an effort to swiftly end the dispute. Furthermore, the *hadith* 'he who is killed while defending his property is a martyr'[57] is also commonly used to justify the highly violent disputes on land or property problems.

It is worth noting that women and children are totally excluded from any form of punishment and any form of violence in tribal or family disputes. Likewise, except for *fidelity* or *honor* issues, no women can be charged with any crime in the system. Thus, women enjoy absolute freedom from punishment of any sort. Women also can neither be interrogated nor be put in prison for any crime. In TRMEs, the killing of an innocent woman or a child is the most disgraceful act; no matter what would be presented is rationale for it.

Thus, people in this system are not used to seeing dead bodies of women and children. That is why alleged indiscriminate air bombardments by US Forces in Afghanistan, which kill many innocent women and children, cause insurmountable agony and thirst for retaliation from the local population in rural Afghanistan. TRME residents in Afghanistan would be very unlikely to recognize that the US is a legitimate power since it dishonorably kills women and children even if the overall US mission is for the residents' own good. The people in rural Afghanistan do not think of the killing of innocent women and children as *collateral damage*. To them seeing the killing of innocent women and children is a shock with everlasting consequences. This reaction must be taken into account when tailoring COIN strategies.

A woman in the TRMEs could be punished if it is determined by the house or tribal elders as the result of the *collective decision* that her behavior demeaned and dirtied the collective honor of the household or the tribe. The rejection of a marriage proposal of the family elders, or an attempt to marry a foreigner without the approval of the elders, adultery, or a unilateral petition for divorce may be considered punishable by honor killing. The decision for the capital punishment is reached collectively in the family, and preferably the brother is chosen by the elders to conduct the honor killing. Since she demeaned the collective honor of the house/tribe, the honor killing is executed publicly to purify the family name. Nonetheless, in case of disagreements or reservations about the crime, or if the family aims to be discreet about the crime for any reason, other ways of killing a female are chosen such as snake or scorpion attacks at night or falling from the roof of the house.

The number of reported honor killings is statistical information that can indicate the extent to which the society in that specific TRME may be socially fragmented. The rise or fall in the numbers of honor killings is also an indicator of the trend of tribalization in the society. For instance, in Northern Iraq, there has been a drastic increase in the numbers of honor killings in the post-Saddam Hussein era since the state's authority has diminished and the influence of the tribal order has accelerated. According to the

---

57 A *hadith* reported from Abdullah bin Amr bin Al-As (Al Bukhari and Muslim-1355): <http://www.witness-pioneer.org/vil/hadeeth/riyad/11/chap235.htm> (accessed 29 June 2009).

UN Assistance for Iraq (UNAMI) report, the number of honor killings increased by 18 percent from 2006 to 2007.[58] In the first six months of 2007, 255 honor killings were reported.[59] A senior police official in the city of Erbil stated to UNAMI that a majority of unnatural deaths among young women were 'honor killings' and at least two deaths were reported daily.[60] Sadly, only 43 people had been arrested and convicted by the Iraqi Security Forces in Northern Iraq from 2000 to 2007.[61]

It is also worth noting that tribal families that leave TRMEs and settle into a more urbanized environment carry the tradition of honor killings into the cities. Since adult family elders are not sufficiently equipped to handle the new challenges coming with the modern and more urbanized environment, they sometimes make an individual decision to kill family members.

Marriage in TRMEs

Marriage in TRMEs has implications for many people and is handled completely by family elders with little input from the individuals who are to marry. Therefore, it looks like a political decision of a group rather than a simple social contract between two individuals. From the socio-economic point of view, marriage promotes the *fertility of females* in the system. It facilitates the cultural objective of having as many children as possible (preferably sons) and as soon as possible. The quicker marriages are arranged and the younger the bride and groom, the better from a cultural viewpoint. From the political point of view, new lineages and long-term alliances can only be established through marriages in the system. For instance, a tribal leader who arranges for his son to marry the daughter of a high profile religious leader can promote his status and political power in the tribal order. Young people succeed in making independent decisions about marriage only in extraordinary and very rare circumstances and after enduring many threats rooted in the household and the tribe. The motto of 'your elders know best what has to be done' is usually accepted and fosters pre-arranged marriages.

The formation of a new family is always a planned event. The marrying couple is chosen carefully by both sides. The family leaders or the tribal leaders can even promise the marriage of two babies during their infancy, known as a *cradle arrangement*. The initiative for marriage always comes from the family of the young man. If it is not a politically pre-arranged marriage dictated by the tribal/village leaders, the active search for a bride is undertaken by the mother, or if she is not alive, by one of the closest female relatives, preferably the eldest sister. It is always preferred to choose

---

58 <http://www.uniraq.org/FileLib/misc/HR%20Report%20Apr%20Jun%202007%20EN.pdf> p.14.
59 Ibid, p.15.
60 Ibid, p.15.
61 Ibid, p.16.

a *good bride for the house* rather than a *good wife for the husband*. Since it is important to maintain the kinship, cross-cousin marriages are considered the most desirable. This also enables the family to keep their land under the collective control of the family/tribe and prevent the land from being portioned among inter-family or inter-tribe marriages. Aside from being the best option for the elders in the family/tribe, the female paternal cousin has always been the predominant 'love figure' for the young males in TRMEs. A rejection of a marriage proposal by the family of the paternal cousin can lead to an unpleasant reaction in TRMEs.

The bride price, *kalym* or *baslik* money, which is a common phenomenon in TRMEs, is paid by the groom to the family of the bride before the marriage, as payment made in return for the bride's family's loss of her labor and fertility within her kin group. This money justified as a price paid for the dowry, covers the wedding costs and is the sole means to furnish the rooms or house in which the newly married couple will live. Likewise, this money would be used for the celebration of the circumcision (*sunnet*) of the boy in the bride's family. This money is usually paid by the man's father, incurring a debt that the son pays off by working submissively for his father. It is mainly for this reason that an economically dependent son cannot divorce his wife without his father's approval.

After the marriage, all the wives of the household have to be in continuous contact with their future mother-in-law. The marriage of the youngest son is the most sensitive to arrange, since the youngest son does not have the formal right to leave his parents because of the responsibility to care for his parents.

The upbringing of girls in the household begins early, at the age of seven or eight, when they begin to be taught all the necessary skills in the house. Before her marriage, she must know how to; bake bread, prepare food, sew, clean the house, take care of the livestock, spin wool, and cultivate the land. The fact that feeding and rearing a daughter means the family is feeding a worker for someone else's family means that they must get as much work out of the girl as they can during her stay in the parental home. Meanwhile, the living condition of a boy in the family is significantly better. He enjoys the attention and concern of his parents because he is their future supporter and helper.

Infertility is a curse in the TRMEs. An infertile woman is alienated from the house since her inability to have children is considered a divine punishment. Domestic remedies like visiting shrines or religious leaders, or traditional folk medicines, are usually applied first. If all those attempts are unsuccessful, the husband has two options, to divorce his wife or to conduct a second marriage without divorce. If the husband chooses to divorce, and if the divorcee is lucky, her parents would still be able to accommodate her in their house when she returns from her ex-husband's home.

Generally, the amount of *kalum* money paid to the father of the bride is high. Men, therefore, must work for five to 10 years in order to garner sufficient economic resources to obtain a bride. Women, therefore, are usually much younger than their husbands. Brides are usually in their middle to late teens, while grooms are in their mid-20s or even mid-30s. Under these circumstances, cases of widowhood are seen as very common in the tribal order.

It should also be stressed that the marriages between different ethnic and religious groups are highly rare in the tribal order. For the tribesmen, marriages are one of the most important kinship expressions of ethnicity. That is why, intra-tribe marriages have played a great role in keeping the tribal or ethnic identity intact for centuries. Hazaras, for instance, the largest predominantly *Shia* groups in Afghanistan, have been very successful in preserving their tribal and ethnic identity mainly due to the rare occurrences of inter-tribe marriages.

Conclusion

At the age of globalization, in which ideas, goods, and people have become incorporated through a global network of communication, transportation, and trade, the number and speed of inputs to every social system are growing at a rapid rate. That is why, in a globalized world, every society requires mechanisms of social change that not only enable the digestion of inputs but also regulates the society in a timely manner. Most social systems have mechanisms to regulate and govern change such as the elections in democratic societies. These mechanisms set or develop a tempo of change. The ability to adapt quickly to the new environment shaped by inputs seems to be the first and foremost mechanism which determines the resiliency of societies. When this mechanism, which enables society to manage change, no longer functions, a society is then, in a state of disequilibrium. A state of disequilibrium may be defined as a state of an extreme value-new environment imbalance that cannot be regulated by the existing mechanisms of the given society – the superstructure in TRMEs case. The consequences of this disequilibrium not only affect the physical component of the given society, but also cause a value-environment conflict in the mental and emotional component. When the new environment shaped by exogenous inputs does not correspond to the traditional norms and values of the given society, then there would be primarily two options. The first alternative is to change the environment as close to the values and norms of the given society. The second alternative is to change the traditional norms and values so as to adapt to the new environment. If new environment value system conflict cannot be addressed with a proper strategy, systemic pressures in the society would eventually lead to frustration, either deprivation or ideological based.

Currently, the inputs exposed into rural Afghanistan, for instance, have been flowing both from extremism and foreign presence – two symbiotic sources of inputs, in fact, which feed each other. Modernity has currently been coming to rural Afghanistan either as the form of reformist *Salafi/Wahhabi* understanding or deviant consequences of foreign presence. *Salafism/Wahhabism* entices many in rural Afghanistan and many more TRMEs in the globe since it proposes a socio-political system that institutionally rejects change and adaptation, or the concept of *ictihad*.[62] *Salafism/Wahhabism*

---

62 *Ictihad* is defined as an Islamic scholarly process of adopting Islamic belief to changing time and circumstances.

argues that Islam is purely and inherently perfect and any attempt to change or reformulate Islam is an attempt to subvert God's will. Stated another way, *Salafi/Wahhabi* movements argue that the main cause of the current turmoil and deprivation prevalent in TRMEs is the 'excessive modernization', or bombardment of the superstructure with earthly exogenous inputs, or *bid'as*. The tenets of *Salafism/Wahhabism*, which create a sort of 'cult of nostalgia' and breed the emotion of 'missing old beautiful days', perfectly fits to close-inflexible social systems designed to resist social evolution such as TRMEs. Though *Salafi/Wahhabi* indoctrination is a reactionary modernist one with a distinct political agenda, their rhetoric of correcting the 'spoiled environment with earthly inputs' to restructure it according to the traditional value system, or *akhlaq*, in rural Afghanistan perfectly fits the needs of many. In contrast, the alliance of the corrupted tribal order, government officials and foreigners, which may seem to be the primary cause of the spoiled environment for many in rural Afghanistan, challenges to the tenets of the value system, or moral codes of behavior, or *akhlaq*. This challenge, thus, alienates the 'frustrated majority' while the rejoicing 'happy minority' benefits from aligning with the foreigners.

2

Afghanistan: A View from the Ground

> Come, come again, whoever you are, come!
> Heathen, fire worshipper or idolatrous, come!
> Come even if you broke your penitence a hundred times,
> Ours is the portal of hope, not the portal of despair, come as you are.
>
> Mawlana Rumi, 13th century Islamic Scholar and Sufi

Although Islam came to Afghanistan 1,100 years ago, rural Afghanistan has been a tribal society for roughly 5,000 years. Tribal and rural structures in Afghanistan, therefore, precede Islam. For instance, the army of Alexander the Great – an undefeated hi-tech army the equivalent of a Western superpower – and its legendary campaign against the local tribes in Afghanistan (330-327 BC) has inspired military historians for centuries. While scholars today underline interesting similarities between the campaign of Alexander the Great and the current fight of the Coalition Forces in Afghanistan, the dates of the campaigns point to a key difference.[1] The army of Alexander the Great, which was a pre-Christian Western power, fought local tribes in Afghanistan, which were pre-Islamic societies, without religious motivations on either side. The common characteristic, which exists both in the campaign of Alexander the Great and the current war in Afghanistan, is not religion, but *tribal and rural order.*

Why has the population in rural Afghanistan been responding to the efforts of the CF and central government in Kabul with determination and tenacity? The answer to this question is not solely Islam as we have seen in the case of Alexander the Great, but it lies in the many aspects of tribal and rural Afghanistan; its terrain features and weather conditions, population structures, traditions, tribal structures and ethnicity, the nature of Afghan family and kin groups in rural areas, and gender roles etc.

---

1   Frank L. Holt, *Into the Land of Bones: Alexander the Great in Afghanistan* (Los Angeles: University of California Press, 2006), p.xi. Also available online: <http://www.books.google.com> (accessed 7 September 2009).

For instance, the ability of the residents of rural Afghanistan to adapt to arid terrain, extreme climatic conditions, prolonged draughts, and successive invasions, would be worth mentioning to explain the roots of their tenacity and determination. The rural Afghanis have also coped with these difficulties by showing diversity, ingeniousness and flexibility in implementing strategies to survive, and by forming impermeable social institutions. Despite certain commonality shared by tribal, rural and religious structures, they have moved from one subsistence strategy to another to adapt to the changing geographic and socio-political environments. That is why geographic, religious, demographic and socio-political features of Afghanistan have favored all insurgencies and contributed a lot to their persistency in the history of Afghanistan. Six major factors contribute to the tenacity of rural Afghanistan. These are:

a) locals in rural Afghanistan are deeply divided along ethnic, linguistic, sectarian and tribal lines, a factor which causes a complex and heterogeneous social terrain that cannot be easily controlled by COIN forces;
b) the social system in rural Afghanistan is based on communal loyalties, which often prevail national identities, and therefore, making Afghanistan a highly decentralized society that cannot be governed from Kabul;
c) the harsh terrain features and weather conditions, when added to the lack of socio-economic development they increase the physical distance between the periphery and the central government;
d) the hard-to penetrate tribal layer makes it merely possible to freely operate in intra-tribe level for COIN forces, a simple fact that destines COIN forces to attain the consent of tribal leaders at all cost and by all means, and thus makes them the passive players in the game;
e) the doctrines of the superstructure, a mechanism formed by the amalgamation of religious principles and traditional local codes, constitute a fertile moral ground of the insurgency, and grant direction and motivation for the insurgents;
f) Afghanistan has a long history of foreign invasions due to its geo-strategic location, as a factor which makes all Afghans genetically expert in guerilla warfare.[2]

These features not only hinder the crafting of a comprehensive and one-size fits all COIN strategy that would be applied anywhere in rural Afghanistan, but also distorts the efforts by disabling the COIN forces to accurately address the center of the gravity of the COIN campaign throughout Afghanistan. Therefore, without citing to the role of these factors in the inability of the central governments and invasion forces to effectively combat and eliminate the insurgencies within the context of the turbulent history of Afghanistan, we may not be able to accurately address the nature of current dilemma.

---

2   Larry P. Goodson, *Afghanistan's Endless War; State Failure, Regional Politic and the Rise of the Taliban* (Seattle: University of Washington Press, 2001), pp.12-14.

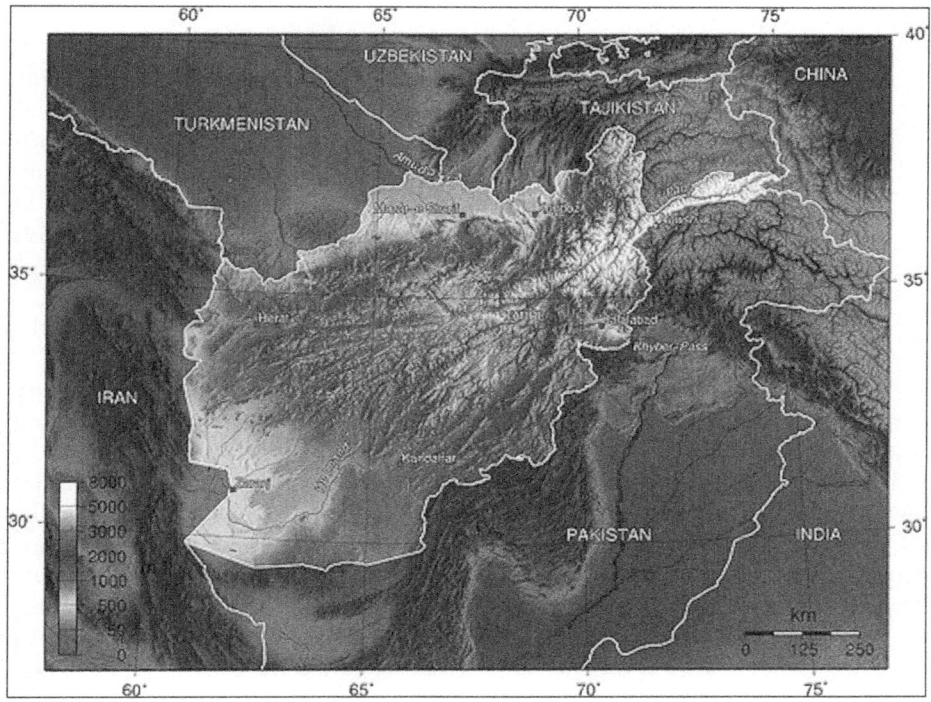

Map 1 Topography of Afghanistan. (<https://www.cia.gov/library/publications/the-world-factbook/geos/af.html> (accessed 10 September 2010))

The Physical Environment and Population

Afghanistan is a landlocked country that occupies a total area roughly equal to the size of the state of Texas and located in South/Central Asia strategically connecting the Asian sub-continent to the energy reserves of the Central Asian states. Afghanistan's border with Pakistan sits astride through difficult terrain for 2,400 kilometers in the South and East; the border has been a great source of tension between the two countries and continues to be a challenge as insurgents use the difficult terrain to infiltrate into and exfiltrate from Afghanistan. Afghanistan also shares its boundaries with China, Iran, Turkmenistan, Uzbekistan, and Tajikistan. Afghanistan's Northern and Western borders are also problematic and generally regarded as transit routes for transnational smuggling.[3]

---

3   Roohullah Rahimi, 'Afghanistan: Exploring the Dynamics of Sociopolitical Strife and Persistency of Insurgency', (Pearson Peacekeeping Centre, Ottawa: Occasional Paper 2,

The Hindu Kush Mountains divide Afghanistan into three major regions:

a) the Central Highlands, which form the Western part of the Himalayan Mountains and accounts for roughly two-thirds of the country's area. Over 50 percent of total land area, therefore, lies above 2,000 meters of Afghanistan. Mountains with dramatic, often spectacular, scenery traverse the center of the country running generally in a Northeast-Southwest direction. The highest peaks are over 7,000 meters and are found in the Eastern part of the country.[4] The mountains diminish in height as they stretch westward;
b) the Southwestern Plateau, which accounts for one-fourth of the land;
c) the smaller Northern Plains area, which contains the country's most fertile soil.

Afghanistan extends over 250,000 square miles, with 70 percent of its territory covered by rugged and high mountain ranges. Only 12 percent of Afghanistan's land is arable.[5] Afghanistan, as a landlocked country, is desperately dependent on the roads, and the nearest sea port is Karachi, in Pakistan, almost 1,000 miles away. Afghanistan, therefore, is mainly dependent upon its neighbors for access to the outside world. The CF cannot sustain its war effort against the insurgents without cooperative neighbors, particularly Pakistan. This source of vulnerability for the CF limits their complete freedom of operations in Afghanistan. Eighty percent of the CF cargo and 40 percent of fuel requirements, for instance, pass through Pakistan.[6] Uzbekistan, its North-West neighbor, has already declined any further support to the CF.[7]

In addition to the mountains, the country also possesses many rivers, which simply empty into arid portions of the country, spending themselves through evaporation, without emptying into another watercourse.

The general climate of the country is typical of arid steppe with very cold winters and dry summers. Summer is usually accompanied by intense heat, drought and sand storms, and thus brings much hardship to the inhabitants in rural areas. Winter is cold and accompanied with heavy snow fall which extremely affects the daily life in rural areas. Nonetheless, historically, the rugged terrain and harsh climate conditions in rural Afghanistan have impeded but not deterred the local population living there.

    2008). Full report: <http://www.peaceoperations.org/wp-content/uploads/2010/02/OP2_Rahimi.pdf>
4 <http://www.globalsecurity.org/military/world/afghanistan/cs-enviro.htm> (accessed 10 September 2010).
5 <http://www.globalsecurity.org/military/world/afghanistan/cs-enviro.htm> (accessed 10 September 2010).
6 Shuja Nawaz, *FATA – A Most Dangerous Place* (Washington D.C.: Center for Strategic & International Studies (CSIS), January 2009), p.1: <http://csis.org/files/media/csis/pubs/081218_nawaz_fata_web.pdf> (accessed 10 January 2010).
7 Ibid.

These geographic factors, in contrast, strengthen their survival skills and reinforce their tenacity.

Before we dig into the other side of the COIN in Afghanistan, it is important to describe some facts about Afghan demography as well. Before the Soviet invasion, there had been only one official census in 1979, which reported that the settled population in the country was 13 million and additional 2.5 million nomads, for a total population of 15.5 million. The census also estimated that only 16 percent of the population lived in urban areas and that about 50 percent of that urban population lived in Kabul.[8] While no credible census has been conducted in Afghanistan to disclose the exact population numbers or ethnic proportions recently, expert estimates are available. According to the *CIA Factbook*, the current population of Afghanistan is around 28.3 million, 76 percent of which live in rural areas as of the year 2010.[9]

Afghanistan is a multi-ethnic and multi-lingual society, reflecting its strategic location spanning historic trade and invasion routes between Western Asia, Central Asia, and Southern Asia. The majority of Afghanistan's population consists of Pashtuns (42 percent) and Tajiks (27 percent). Hazaras (nine percent), Uzbeks (nine percent), Aimak (four percent), Turkmen (three percent), Baluch (two percent) follow Pashtuns and Tajiks. Islam is the religion of 99.7 percent of Afghanistan. An estimated 80 percent of the population practice *Sunni* Islam, following the *Hanafi* School of Jurisprudence; 19 percent is *Shia*.[10] While there are more than 30 different dialects spoken in the country, Dari and Pashto are the two official languages of Afghanistan and used most widely.

The Pashtuns are the dominant ethnic group in Afghanistan today and have always remained the most influential group in rural Afghanistan since the 18th century. Pashtuns are also the largest existing tribal society in the world.[11] The Pashtuns are divided into three main groups. Members of the Durrani tribe, which ruled the country for two centuries, are primarily found North and West of Kandahar.[12] Members of the Ghilzai tribe, who were defeated by the Duranis, are found in the East and North of Afghanistan. All other tribes, representing the third leg of the tribal triangle, are spread throughout Afghanistan and Pakistan.

Geographic and demographic facts stated above, specifically the heterogeneity both in geographic and demographic terms, have led to the creation and preservation of the tribal and rural characteristics in Afghanistan, which is in fact, in favor of tribal order.

---

8 <http://www.globalsecurity.org/military/world/afghanistan/cs-enviro.htm> (accessed 10 September 2010).
9 <https://www.cia.gov/library/publications/the-world-factbook/geos/af.html> (accessed 10 September 2010).
10 <https://www.cia.gov/library/publications/the-world-factbook/geos/af.html> (accessed 10 September 2010).
11 Larry P. Goodson, *Afghanistan's Endless War; State Failure, Regional Politics and the Rise of the Taliban* (Seattle: University of Washington Press, 2001), p.14.
12 Ibid, p.14.

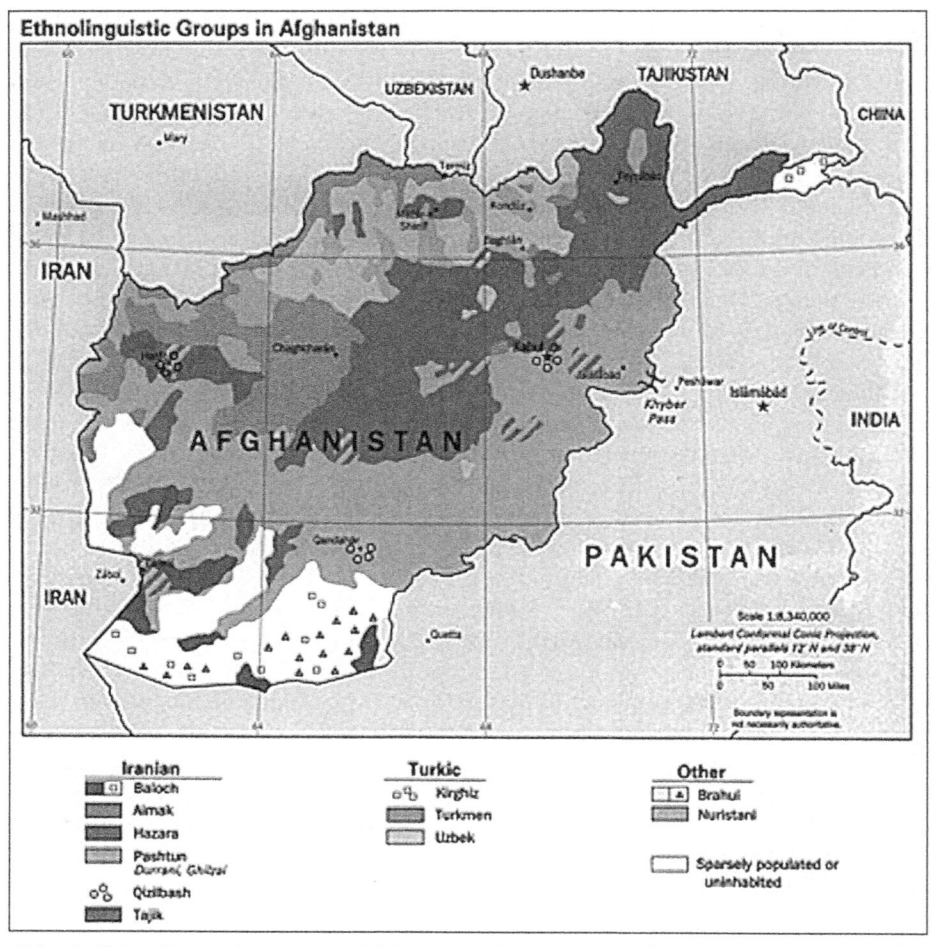

Map 2 Ethnolinguistic groups in Afghanistan. (*Global Security*, 'Afghanistan Maps'. <http://www.globalsecurity.org/military/world/afghanistan/maps.htm> (accessed 13 February 2007))

These facts have also been the primary cause of the failure of the central governments and invading forces to consolidate their control over the entire country throughout the history of Afghanistan. Harsh weather conditions, specifically long and bitter winters, for instance, have made it impossible to conduct a decisive and persistent campaign against the insurgencies, and turned the COIN efforts into seasonal fights, which granted the insurgents the opportunity to rest and regroup.

With respect to the border region between Afghanistan and Pakistan, the land is inhospitable to 'the outsiders' with mountain ranges, narrow valleys, desert plains, and rocky, barren wastes. The physical feature of this land makes it impossible to draw a definable border. Like veins on a leaf, there are hundreds of small valleys in the region, the total control of which are absolutely impossible to count even with aerial surveillance, which perfectly serve as safe corridors for small groups. The difficult terrain of the country coupled with dispersed population settlements renders a great number of people isolated from the urban centers and from each other. While the circle highway built by the Americans and the Soviets in the 1960s connects the urban centers, as well as the population that resides within proximity of the highway, the rest of the population are ill-integrated in the national system. As a result, many of the rural populations are isolated and poorly integrated. Dispersed rural population and the control of which is merely possible, donates safe havens for the insurgents who seek for logistic support, intelligence and recruitment. Furthermore, the isolation of a great section of the population necessitates the rise of alternative forms of support affiliations. The tribal order, as a local governance model, is thus a result of both the experiences of these people within the context of the physical features of their land and the perceived malice of the central authority. This diversity or heterogeneity in the rural society has been further exacerbated due to the legacy of war and external proxy interference over the past three decades.

In the light of the facts stated above, rural Afghan society would be regarded as a complex assortment of ethnic, linguistic, religious and tribal cleavages more intimately united at the local level than under the flag of the 'Afghan' identity at the national level. It should also be stressed that this trend of tribalization/localization is continuing in rural Afghan society in a less intense manner in contributing to the persistence of the insurgency.[13]

In the same vein, one may note that the 'decentralized' nature of insurgency, as an antecedent condition mainly rooted from the varying political aspirations and objectives of different political movements and interest groups, perfectly fits for the continuation of tribal characteristics of the society. Since tribal order would best be characterized as a system of different armed groups with different political agendas, decentralized insurgency would facilitate a fertile ground for the tribal confederates to play their triple roles. That is, the tribal confederates ally with the Taliban, tribal confederates ally with the CF and the ones which sit on the fence and the everlasting flow of switching alliances, which hinders to figure out whose hands are in whose pockets.

What is said about the primary features of the Taliban-led insurgency? In the light of the aforementioned facts stated above, and the map below, which shows the Taliban presence as of the year of 2009 in Afghanistan, what sort of outcomes would be derived? It would be appropriate to pinpoint that the Taliban-led insurgency is, first a tribal one, then a rural one, and lastly a religious one.

---

13   Roohullah Rahimi, 'Afghanistan: Exploring the Dynamics of Sociopolitical Strife and Persistency of Insurgency'.

Map 3 Taliban presence in Afghanistan as of 2015. (<https://www.washingtonpost.com/news/worldviews/wp/2015/10/15/this-map-explains-why-obama-decided-to-leave-thousands-of-troops-in-afghanistan/> (accessed 4 February 2016))

Today Stems from Yesterday

'What is history?' If you ask this question to any Afghan, the answer you would hear would possibly be that 'history is a collection of broken cycles, not a progressive straight line'. Then to better understand the current turmoil in rural Afghanistan, we should focus on why and how the last cycle for Afghanistan was broken and which casual mechanism led to this break.

Mawlana Rumi, the founder of the Sufi Mawlawi School and a famous 13th century Islamic scholar, was born in the city of Belkh in Afghanistan. Belkh is 200 miles North of Kabul and very close to the Nuristan region, in which eight US soldiers were killed in a Taliban raid in their Forward Operation base on 4 October 2009.[14] Mawlana Rumi states in his famous book Mathnawi that 'the lamps [the religions] are different but the Light is the same…' This sentence from 13th century Afghanistan contradicts with Afghanistan today. The question I want to raise in this section is,

---

14 BBC News, 'Heavy US Losses in Afghan War': <http://news.bbc.co.uk/2/hi/8289200.stm> (accessed 26 October 2010).

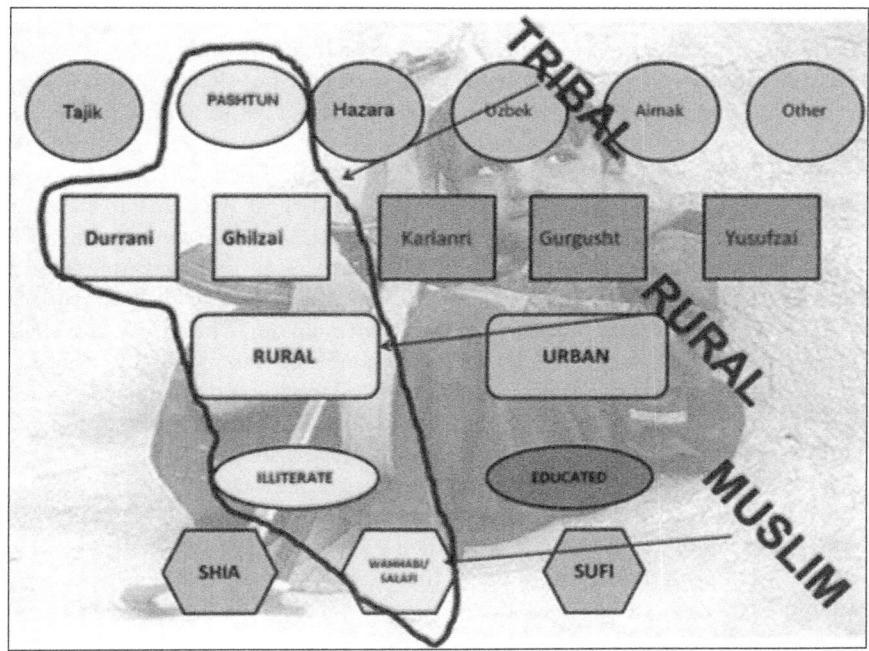

Figure 1 The components of the Taliban-led insurgency. (Author's own illustration)

that while the soil of Afghanistan endowed us, Mawlana Rumi and many Islamic scholars, who were the representative of tolerance, coexistence and peace specifically in 13th century and succeeding centuries, why today, are the grandsons of Mawlana strictly and brutally following an insurgency and are killing innocent people coldbloodedly? Which dynamics led to this transformation, and how could this dilemma be accurately addressed?

In conventional terms, traditional tribal leaders, or *Khans*,[15] make executive decisions which provide justice, security and essential services to their followers as responsive leaders, and justify them with the moral code of behavior, or *akhlaq*, that combines tribal and Islamic values. Appeal to these moral codes by tribal leaders to legitimize their orders in the eyes of their followers is not only a necessity for them in order to maintain their authority but also it is a kind of social contract, tasking them to take care their of tribesmen and to be responsible for them. The title of '*Khan*'

---

15   Gilles Dorronsoro, *Revolution Unending: Afghanistan, 1979 to Present* (Columbia University Press, 2005), p.120. Also available online: <www.google.books.com>

who is a self-financed public servant, expending his own wealth for the good of the community,[16] is given to these caring traditional leaders. The absence of an aggressive central authority and non-violent characteristics of traditional *Sufi* networks in TRMEs, have created enough political space for the *Khans* to govern in TRMEs. In particular, traditional Islamic networks such as *Sufi* orders never sought to apply political violence to challenge the authority of tribal leaders in TRMEs.

This delicate political equilibrium, which governed rural Afghanistan for centuries, started to crumble in the early 1970s, when Afghanistan turned out to be a 'front' in the rivalry between the US and the Soviet Union. Former Prime Minister Mohammad Sardar Daoud Khan, the king's cousin and brother-in-law, overthrew King Zahir Shah and seized power in a non-violent coup on 17 July 1973. A Republic was declared in Afghanistan and Daoud, who abolished the monarchy, decided to title himself president instead of king. President Daoud was a staunch nationalist, upon assuming power he ended the monarchy and declared Afghanistan a Republic; within the context of the Cold War he enjoyed close relations with the Soviet Union and heavily depended on Soviet aid.

Under Daoud, certain liberalization took place, meaning that some of the most draconian realities of the monarchy were rolled back, but by and large whatever hopes and expectations arose among the people – little was done to satisfy them. Specifically, his attempts to carry out badly-needed economic and social reforms were met with little success, and the new constitution promulgated in February 1977 failed to quell chronic political instability.

Daoud had seized power with the help of an underground party named the People's Democratic Party of Afghanistan (PDPA) – a pro-Moscow communist party. Once he had consolidated power though and felt he no longer needed these controversial allies, he ditched them, and most of the PDPA members were arrested with his order shortly after. Nonetheless, Hafizullah Amin and a number of military wing officers of the PDPA's Khalq faction (more independent from Moscow than the Babrak Karmal-led Parcham faction) managed to remain at large and organize an uprising.

In 1978, Nur Mohammad Taraki, Babrak Karmal and Amin Taha led the PDPA, carried out a military coup, known as the Saur Revolution, and overthrew the regime of Mohammad Daoud, who was assassinated along with all of his family members.

The root causes for the present conflict in the country can be traced back to this momentous event. The military officers behind the coup handed power to their PDPA leaders. The Marxist party embarked on a set of ambitious reforms geared towards eliminating the tribal social structure in rural areas, as well as bringing much needed economic development to the country. After seizing power they began a series of limited reforms, such as declaring, more or less, a secular state. They moved to replace religious and traditional laws with secular and Marxist ones. They sought to curtail

---

16   Barnett R. Rubin, *The Fragmentation of Afghanistan* (London: Yale University Press, 2002), p.43.

the practice of purchasing brides, and tried to implement an ambitious land reform program, nationalizing and redistributing the lands, waiving farmers' debts countrywide and banning traditional practices. Men were also obliged to cut their beards, women couldn't wear a *burqa*, and mosques were placed off limits.

The majority of people in the cities, including Kabul, either welcomed or were ambivalent to these policies. However, the secular nature of the government made it unpopular with conservative Afghans in the countryside, who advocated the traditional moral codes of behavior, *or akhlaq*, and thought that these new policies challenged *the superstructure*. Tribal leaders, who lost their privileges in the land reform, had been at odds with the policies of Kabul as well.

These reform efforts of the PDPA, as an 'illegitimate and un-Islamic government', were severely criticized by newly emerged Islamists as well at Kabul University, the majority of whom were comprised by polarized rural young men from the Pashtuns' Ghilzai tribal confederation and aimed at the creation of an Islamic state and largely affected by the Muslim Brotherhood and Jamaat-i Islami Party. Specifically, following the *Saur* or April Revolution in 1978, Islam was drastically transformed into the primary resistance ideology and the policies of the PDPA were agitated by these newly emerged young Islamists as a threat to the Islamic identity of the country.

The critiques of rural Afghans, tribal leaders and Islamists turned into a fierce political opposition very soon. The PDPA's response to this was very heavy-handed, aggravating the situation. Leaders of Islamist opposition fled to Pakistan and declared *Jihad* to claim the leadership of Afghan resistance. They also received all covert aid from the US via Pakistan. While the US regarded these Islamists as a new political card to contain the communist ideology in the region, Pakistan viewed them as strengthening her hand against the sensitive issue of Pashtunistan, the irredentist cause of reuniting the Pashtuns which was championed by Daoud to enjoy the support of many domestic groups including the Pashtun tribes.

Soon several rural areas rose in open armed rebellion against the communist government. This was the initial alliance of tribal order and Islamists against the central government in Kabul, which was the representative of corrupted political order aimed at defying the superstructure. Consequently, in 1979, with the Afghan Army unable to cope with the large number of violent incidents when faced with the defeat of the PDPA which meant the erosion of global credibility of communist ideology, the Soviet Union decided to invade Afghanistan.[17]

Though, perhaps, this was not the Soviets' original intent, once inside Afghanistan, they found themselves forced to commit more and more troops and material to prop up the unpopular PDPA government. On 25 December 1979, the Soviet Army entered Kabul. This was the starting point of the Soviet occupation, which ended only in 1989 with a full withdrawal of Soviet troops under the Geneva Accords which was reached

---

17 Anthony Arnold, *Afghanistan's Two-Party Communism: Parcham and Khalq* (Stanford: Hoover Press, 1983).

in 1988 between Afghanistan and Pakistan. This historic event was to be the inception of a three-decade long turmoil in Afghanistan.

The Soviet invasion changed the dimension of the conflict in Afghanistan from internal power squabbles to an international crisis premised on ideological differences and imperial ambitions. Immediately after the Soviet invasion, the resistance to the Soviet presence began with desertions from the Afghan Army and an open revolt inside the country. In the meantime, the Western bloc led by the US, declared intentions to aid the Afghan resistance against the Soviet occupation of Afghanistan.

The Afghan resistance, in fact, was initially comprised of various groups including Islamists and nationalists; however, the Islamists became more dominant in the struggle over the course of time. The composition of the groups constantly fluctuated, until seven main groups emerged, four of which were Islamists and three traditionalists. In broad terms, the difference between the two groups was that 'Islamists were radical in outlook, and regarded their struggle as primarily one for a state and society fashioned in accordance with Islamic principles, while the traditionalists saw it primarily as a struggle for national liberation. Thus the latter were willing to see a return of King Zahir, but the former regarded a monarchy as un-Islamic'.[18]

The prevalent turmoil before and during the Soviet invasion in Afghanistan led to drastic socio-political and economic outcomes, most of which functioned as antecedent conditions in the process of the emergence of the Taliban. First, the Soviet invasion of Afghanistan and the counter-strategies applied by the US-led coalition against this invasion declined the numbers of responsive *Khans* in TRMEs and turned most of them into unapproachable *warlords*, who selfishly seek fame, political and military power. Second, Islam, the most important commonality in this diverse country, was chosen as the most obvious mobilizer against the Soviet invasion.[19] The construction of an identity which would unite all Afghanis for the same cause with the mobilization of Islam could be the best way to exploit this commonality. In 1984, according to the then CIA Director, William Casey, 'there were many Muslims in the Soviet CIA [and in Afghanistan] and they could do a lot of damage to the Soviet Union by carrying out the battle to their own turf since Islam was an antidote to the spread of Communism'.[20] Nonetheless, the problem before this grand strategy was the lenient characteristics of the main indigenous Islamic versions practiced in Afghanistan. Pakistan/Saudi sponsored and *Wahhabi/Salafi* indoctrinated and armed *Jihad* with a distinct political agenda which would perfectly serve for the political ambitions of the US-led coalition to stop the spread of communism in Afghanistan and in the region. The Reagan administration regarded the possibility of mobilizing one billion Muslims against what President Reagan called the 'Evil Empire' as a

---

18 Sir Martin Ewans, *Afghanistan: A New History* (London: Routledge, Curzon, 2002), p.155.
19 John K. Cooley, *Unholy Wars: Afghanistan, America and International Terrorism*, 3rd edition (London: Pluto Press, 2002), p.xv.
20 Adeep Khalid Ibid, p.116.

'God-sent opportunity'.²¹ During a reception at the White House, President Reagan is on record describing the Mujahideen as the moral equivalent of the US Founding Fathers thanks to their role against the 'Evil Empire'.²²

Though the mainstream *Hanafi* School regards this 'armed version of *Jihad*' as the lesser one, which must be implemented under the strict control of Islamic Law and the supervision of scholars to defend the invaded country, the spiritual consequence of this 'predatory' strategy was the arrival of this new radicalized and militarized Islamic doctrine to Afghanistan. The radical and armed version of Islam would perfectly provide to the objective of denying the expansion of communism at all costs and by all means. Could the Mujahideen with Quran in one hand and an AK-47 in the other, serve for this objective? Unfortunately, the answer of Western world was to be 'yes' to this question.

In material terms, whereas the Carter administration began support for the resistance, the Reagan Doctrine of driving the Soviets from Afghanistan 'by all means available'²³ pushed the flow of cash to the resistance in Afghanistan to $630 million in 1987.²⁴ While US aid spent $30.2 million on education in Afghanistan from 1986-1990, and billions of dollars flowed mainly from the US and the Middle East to Afghanistan to support the Mujahideen and their holy *Jihad*, which had then a unifying potency among people.²⁵ US cash to the Mujahideen was almost $5 billion in the period from 1980-1989.²⁶ The total expenditure of the Soviets, on the other hand, was $5 billion per year ($45 billion in total), and yet they lost.²⁷

Without considering the political and socio-economic dynamics involved in Afghanistan, the Western world called for a unity under the roof of the armed *Jihad* against the infidel communists as a short-term objective with long-term unintended consequences. At this point, the question I want to raise is: what happened to those Mujahideens? In guerilla warfare, one of the missions of the Special Forces is to train the friendly guerilla forces fighting against the hostile regime. The last phase of the guerilla warfare is *demobilization*, by far the most important among all phases. It would be applied as two techniques. The first one is to transform the guerilas into the standing national army. The Kosovo Liberation Army or resistance in Bosnia would

---

21   Eqbal Ahmad, 'Terrorism: Theirs and Ours' in *Terrorism and Counterterrorism: Understanding the New Security Environment: Readings & Interpretations*, 39-49. Editors Russell D. Howard, and Reid L. Sawyer, Rev. and updated ed. (Guilford, Conn: McGraw-Hill/Dushkin, 2004), p.39.
22   Ibid.
23   Barnett R. Rubin, *The Fragmentation of Afghanistan* (London: Yale University Press, 2002), p.181.
24   Ibid, p.181.
25   Ahmed Rashid, *Taliban: Militant Islam, Oil, and Fundamentalism in Central Asia* (London: Yale University Press, 2001), p.18.
26   Mike Bowker, *Russia, America and Islamic World* (Asghate, 2007), p.35. Also available online: <www.google.books.com>
27   Ahmed Rashid, *Taliban: Militant Islam, Oil, and Fundamentalism in Central Asia*, p.18.

be stated as a good example of this strategy. The second one is to integrate the guerillas into the civilian life by providing them with decent job opportunities. This is the treacherous side of demobilization because as the time passes in protracted insurgency, being a warrior would become a job for a guerilla who participated in the movement. It is unlikely for anyone to expect from an individual who carried an AK-47 rifle for years, to work from 8:00 a.m. to 5:00 p.m. and adapt himself to the routines of daily life without any rehabilitation program that addresses socio-physiological and economic issues. Neither of these two options of the demobilization was the case for Afghanistan after the Soviet withdrawal in 1989. After the Soviets, the Western world withdrew from Afghanistan as well without properly addressing the demobilization phase of the Mujahideens. The victory over communism in Afghanistan made the Western world so blind that they could not appreciate the demobilization phase. The Mujahideen were forgotten in Afghanistan with the Quran in one hand, and AK-47 in the other and question marks in their minds with what to do next. Unfortunately, right now the current dilemma we face is mainly rooted from these question marks. The answers of the Mujahideen leaders to the questions about what to do next after the withdrawal of the Soviets and the Western world from Afghanistan were to be the grassroots of the current dilemma in Afghanistan. Regrettably, the immediate loss of interest in the region by the Western world after the Soviet withdrawal can be considered one of the major causes of the extremists' triumph in post-Soviet Afghanistan.

As aid of all sorts increased, mainly cash and military equipment, during the Soviet invasion, the Mujahideen leaders, who would, in fact, play traditional the '*Khan*' role, became less dependent on the local population and less responsive to the traditional tribal order.[28] They withdrew from tribal social life by moving out from their houses and by starting to live in well-fortified bases. This was the start of their transformation from Mujahideen leaders into warlords.[29] These newly emerged warlords, with the strength of foreign money and foreign arms, initiated an unprecedented civil war in rural Afghanistan. The traditional rural economy that had sustained the TRMEs collapsed due to prolonged war, and tribal leaders could no longer rely on the traditional economy to finance their need for more sophisticated warfare capabilities such as heavy artillery and tanks to deter adversaries. They turned their backs on those they governed, ignoring the superstructure and the tribal order, because they thought that the easy money coming from the foreigners, and the profits from smuggling, robbery, kidnapping, drug/arms trafficking would be enough to rule. These newly emerged warlords and the corrupt circles around them not only caused drastic fluctuations to the delicate social balance in TRMEs, but also spoiled the peaceful co-operation of

---

28 George Crile, *Charlie Wilson's War: The Extraordinary Story of How the Wildest Man in Congress and a Rogue CIA Agent Changed the History of Our Times* (New York: Grove Press, 2003), pp.474-478.
29 Ahmed Rashid, *Descent into Chaos* (London: Penguin Books, 2008), p.125. Also, Chapter Seven of the book, called 'The One-Billion-Dollar Warlords'.

the tribal leaders and the traditionally non-violent Islamic networks in Afghanistan. Ahmed Rashid explicitly addresses this grim fact of the rising warlord order, which turned out to be an official government strategy of the Bush administration just after 2003, by stating that 'Rumsfeld's determination to legalize warlord authority against the wishes of the Afghan government and people was the most fatal mistake he was to make'.[30]

In the following years of Soviet withdrawal in 1989, Afghanistan, left alone by the international community, went down a brutal civil war between rival Mujahideen factions. During the Soviet invasion, except for the mutual hostility of these factions to the Russians and the Kabul regime, the resistance groups had little in common. Though these groups were more inclined to co-operate than to fight each other during the invasion, the bleak civil war period after the Soviet invasion proved that not even their shared Islamic faith, nor the binding concept of *Jihad* was strong enough to outweigh their personal, ethnic, tribal, and sectarian differences.

Following the withdrawal of Soviet troops, the Najibullah government survived the onslaught of the Afghan resistance forces due to the massive aid that the regime continued to receive from the Soviet Union, but more importantly because of the inability of the resistance groups to form a united front against the government. Divisions among the resistance groups existed since their inception, these divisions intensified as the defeat of the Kabul regime became more eminent. The defeat of the Najibullah government in 1992 and the failure of the resistance groups to agree on a political settlement led to a vicious power struggle which culminated in urban warfare and the division of Afghanistan into zones of influence among resistance commanders. Nonetheless, the defeat the Najibullah government caused the beginning of a new episode both for Afghanistan and international community. The 9/11 attacks drastically increased the visibility of Afghanistan as a front against global extremism as it was a base for the al-Qaeda networks. That is why, soon after the 9/11 attacks the international community unanimously responded to the threat of global extremism. On 12 September 2001, the UN Security Council announced its:

> ... support for the efforts of the Afghan people to replace the Taliban regime, while condemning for allowing Afghanistan to be used as a base for terrorism and for providing safe haven to Osama bin Laden, and authorized the member

---

30 Ibid, p.127. Another quote from the book: 'In the midst of the Taliban summer offensive [in 2004], the Afghan government also had to contend with fighting between warlords in the West and the North. Yet in August 2004 Wolfowitz asked Congress to authorize $500 million for training and equipping local security forces- not just armies- to counter terrorism and insurgencies. The Pentagon wanted to hire warlords in Yemen, Pakistan, and Somalia to combat al Qaeda because it considered that its warlord strategy had worked so well in Afghanistan. It was an insult to the Afghanis who had suffered so much under the warlords', p.254.

states – under Chapter VII of the Charter of the United Nations – to take appropriate measures to tackle with international system...[31]

In addition to the response of the UN, NATO invoked Article 5 for the first time and 'declared its solidarity with the US and pledged its support and assistance'.[32] With the broad support of the international community, the US government led an international coalition that was formed to topple the Taliban regime. This coalition closely co-operated with local opposition forces and entered Kabul with the support of the main opposition Northern Alliance's militia forces within eight weeks of the start of the attacks. Soon later, the CF waged war against the Taliban under the umbrella of Operation Enduring Freedom (OEF). On 27 November 2001, the international community and all parties, including the opposition movements against the Taliban, gathered in Bonn under the UN supervision. At the end of the meeting, all parties agreed to start the Bonn process, which was built on three pillars: political reform, securing the environment, and reconstruction of the country.[33] The Bonn Agreement largely consisted of a political framework that stressed the need for a highly centralized government. Hamid Karzai was designated chairman of the Afghan Interim Authority. Following this appointment, Karzai requested that the UN send forces to Afghanistan on behalf of the authority. As of December 2001, expectations for the future of Afghanistan were relatively positive. Essentially, soon after the Bonn Process and the formation of the central government in Kabul, international military forces – Combined Forces Command-Afghanistan (or CFC-A), International Security Assistance Force (or ISAF) and Afghan security partners – started to deal with the security issues in Afghanistan. In the meantime, ISAF was deployed in Afghanistan under UN Security Council mandate and UN command, yet the ISAF mission was limited to Kabul and Bagram Air Base. In August 2003, the command of ISAF was also handed over to NATO. After the expansion of the area of operation of the ISAF forces in 2006, the number reached to its peak level around 50,000 troops from 42 countries, including all NATO members.[34]

When all of this was happening in Kabul and in the capitals of countries which formed the coalition, what was happening in rural Afghanistan, which, unfortunately, was completely forgotten by the international community from the end of Soviet invasion to 2006? The short answer to this question is: the Taliban was consolidating its power in rural Afghanistan in the five-year long period. The Taliban successfully presented itself by establishing a political authority more legitimate than the corrupted

---

31 *UNSC Resolution 1368*. Full text: <http://daccessdds.un.org> (accessed 1 November 2010).
32 Adgar Buckley, 'Invocation of Article 5: Five years on', *NATO Review* (Summer 2006).
33 Christopher Freeman, 'Introduction: Security Governance and State Building in Afghanistan', *International Peacekeeping*, Vol.14, No.1, (January 2007), p.1.
34 *NATO ISAF Document*, 'NATO's Role in Afghanistan': <http//www.nato.int/cps/en/natolive/topics_8189.htm> (accessed 1 November 2010).

warlord order, or its sole rival in rural Afghanistan, and was more respectful of the superstructure in rural Afghanistan. The Taliban movement, or the most profound unintended consequence of the efforts to transform rural Afghanistan to better fight against communism ideologically, emerged in war-torn rural Afghanistan as an alternative Islamic solution to the problems in rural Afghanistan.[35]

As the Mujahideen groups and warlords were fighting each other for more power in the post-invasion period, Saudi Arabia heavily funded *madrassas* (religious schools) in Pakistan to spread the *Wahhabi* indoctrination in the region. The fractions of Pakistan's *Jamati Islami* started building the *Deobandi* network, an indigenous school of Islam which also includes extremist ideas, to extend their area of influence to Afghanistan. These *madrassas* serving as an educational alternative for thousands of Afghan refugees who had no food and shelter and, for poor Pakistani families who could not afford expensive government schools, played a great role in the expansion of *Wahhabi* and *Deobandi* schools throughout rural Afghanistan and the tribal border line between Afghanistan and Pakistan. With the support of Pakistani military intelligence agency, which aimed to balance the power of old Mujahideen leaders such as Gulbaddin Hikmatyar and the Tajik/Uzbek fractions in the North, these newly fostered networks turned out to be more or less a coherent Islamist movement.

In the following years after the capture of Kabul in 1996, while newly emerged warlords were being alienated from the people and the tribal order, the *madrassa* networks and the mosques were staffed by new religious elites of the Taliban movement. These newly emerged religious classes, who became more autonomous in the warlord-dominated rural Afghanistan and linked with international networks in Pakistan and *Wahhabists*, deviated from their traditional role in TRMEs and openly announced that they wanted political power to rule for the sake of Islam. The Taliban, mainly by means of already existing and highly revered mosque and *madrassa* networks, could rapidly reach anywhere in rural Afghanistan with no confrontation, and it received some popular support during its initial advances from 1994-95.[36] According to Barnett Rubin, when many Mujahideen commanders in TRMEs had become virtual warlords and started to extort tribute from anybody in the area they controlled with brute force, a group of *madrassa* teachers and students led by *Mullah* Muhammad Omar formed the Taliban to end the power of these warlords and establish a cleaner social system.[37] This new rhetoric which enticed the people in TRMEs, together with military aid

---

35 Barnett R. Rubin, *The Fragmentation of Afghanistan* (London: Yale University Press, 2002), p.xiii.
36 David B. Edwards, *Before Taliban: Genealogies of the Afghan Jihad* (Los Angeles: University of California Press, 2002), pp.297-298.
37 Barnett R. Rubin, *The Fragmentation of Afghanistan* (London: Yale University Press, 2002), p.xii.

received from Pakistan, enabled them initially to seize control of Qandahar province in 1994 and to expand until their control to the rest of the country by August 1998.[38]

I should stress that in the Taliban's solution for rural Afghanistan, there was no room for any form of hierarchy including the tribal leaders within the Muslim community.[39] For instance, *Mullah* Muhammad Omar is neither one of the tribal leaders (*Khan* class) or from the royal family of the Muhammadzai branch of the Durrani tribe. He is one of these *Talibs* (students) with high ideals of selflessness, righteousness and piety, or *taqwa*. Superiority could only be obtained by *taqwa*, which means getting closer to God through worshipping and always being conscientious in the application of God's rules.[40] For instance, the Holy Quran dictates that 'The noblest among all human beings are those who possess taqwa (righteousness)'.[41] Similarly, on the occasion of the final pilgrimage, during his last sermon, Prophet Muhammad says that:

> ... there is no superiority of any Arab over any non-Arab or of any non-Arab over any Arab; or of white over black or of black over white. All human beings are the progeny of Adam and Adam was made of dust. The best of you are those who have the most taqwa. If there is superiority in anyone it is due to his God-fearing qualities...[42]

Therefore, *taqwa*, proposed as a criterion of superiority in the social system by the Taliban, fits well with the people in rural Afghanistan, who were already devout Muslims and who strictly followed the principles of Islam. That is, all Muslims in a society are entitled to equal social status and equal rights. The acceptance of the *taqwa* understanding, which opposes any kind of caste system within Islam and dynastic/tribal privileges in the community, by the locals one more time led to the emergence of a 'charismatic *mullah* movement'. Put simply, the Soviet invasion and the prolonged civil war experienced after hindered power of old, influential families, caused the decline of the *Khan* class and the collapse of the traditional pacifist *Sufi* networks in rural areas. The Mujahideen, who successfully drove the Soviets out, failed to establish a new social order to please the rural Afghans, and thus, were alienated by many for not bringing peace and justice to war weary Afghanistan. Traditional society in rural Afghanistan, then, returned to ethnic and tribal divisions. More importantly, the *mullah* class with the rhetoric of purifying the society from all earthly deviations raised as a type of 'believer-warrior'.

---

38 Ahmed Rashid, *Taliban: Militant Islam, Oil, and Fundamentalism in Central Asia* (New Haven: Yale University Press, 2000), p.32.
39 Michael Griffin, *Reaping the Whirlwind: The Taliban Movement in Afghanistan* (London: Pluto Press, 2001), p.55.
40 The word '*Taqwa*' has been mentioned in the Holy Quran 251 times in many verses. This large number of verses related to *taqwa* is an indication of the importance of the subject.
41 *Holy Quran*, Surat Al-Hujurat, Verse: 13.
42 *Sahih Bukhari*, Vol. 7, Ch. 3.

For the first time in the history of Afghanistan, in fact, a political movement has been claiming to govern TRMEs by exploiting Islamic rhetoric for political mobilization. Ahmed Rashid states that:

> [The Taliban] fitted nowhere in the Islamic spectrum of ideas and movements that had emerged in Afghanistan between 1979 and 1994. The Taliban represented nobody but themselves and they recognized no Islam except their own. Before the Taliban, Islamic extremism had never flourished in Afghanistan.[43]

This Islamic extremism, which had never flourished in Afghanistan before, was not only a direct challenge to the tribal order but also the end of the peaceful co-existence of modified Islam and traditional tribal codes under the roof of the superstructure. Interestingly, if we recognize that a typical TRME rejects everything that belongs to the outside and treats it with hostility, we must ask why so many people of rural Afghanistan easily embraced the indoctrination of political networks based on extremist Islamic rhetoric, which is undeniably an alien phenomenon imported from the outside world. Why have many rural Afghans accepted the imported extremist Islam of the Taliban but at the same time preferred to keep themselves at a distance from the options of democracy, governing of the state, or rule of law and all other alien innovations imported by the international efforts in rural Afghanistan? An obvious possibility may be 'the collective fear' of the Taliban. Since the Taliban spreads a 'culture of fear' among people, they may be reluctantly forced to obey to the strict rules of the Taliban. Since this phenomenon of 'culture of fear' is pumped by the Western media with the photographs or footage of the Taliban beating woman with sticks, public executions, and acid attacks, we are very inclined to buy this argument without questioning. Nonetheless, for me, 'culture of fear' is not sufficient enough to answer the question of why the Taliban entices people in rural Afghanistan. Another answer could be the Taliban's rhetoric of fixing and purifying the superstructure and re-establishing moral codes of behavior, or *akhlaq*. Then, the emergence of this rhetoric as an alternative governance model to a highly corrupted warlord order in rural Afghanistan entices many people towards the Taliban. With this rhetoric:

a) The Taliban promises people that its utmost aim is to fix the superstructure and clean it from bad innovations, or *bid'a*. For the Taliban, the current turmoil in Afghanistan is because of excessive modernity and all exogenous inputs, *bid'a* coming with it. Therefore, the only way to fix the structure is to purify it from these exogenous inputs coming with the modernity. These inputs that currently exist in rural Afghanistan contradict with the concept of *akhlaq*, or value system of the society. The only option, then, is to change to resolve this disequilibrium. At the individual level, when the facts in the environment do not correspond

---

43 Ahmed Rashid, *Taliban: Militant Islam, Oil and Fundamentalism in Central Asia*, p.93.

to how one believes one has basically two options. First, one may change the environment and bring our physical condition as close to his/her values, *akhlaq* in this case, as possible. Second, one may change his/her values to adapt to the environment. The former one, which best fits for the objectives of the locals in rural Afghanistan, is currently represented by the Taliban;

b) The Taliban upholds the golden past and creates a cult of nostalgia, which perfectly fits for the mindset of rural Afghans;

c) In the Taliban's solution there was no room for any form of hierarchy including the tribal leaders within the Muslim community. Superiority could only be obtained by the concept of *taqwa* (piety), which means getting closer to God through worshipping and being always conscientious in the application of God's rules. Therefore, *taqwa*, proposed as a criterion of superiority in the social system by the Taliban, fits well with the people in rural Afghanistan, who were already more devout Muslims than the urban people. The motto of 'equality for all, and superiority solely through *taqwa*' entices an ordinary rural Afghan, who has no title in the social life. *Mullah* Omar, once an ordinary rural person and now *emir-al mu'minin* (the leader of all Muslims in Afghanistan), is a good example to prove how the concept of *taqwa* elevates individuals;

d) By offering 'a just political order' and placing the notion of justice above all considerations, the Taliban easily wins the hearts and minds of the rural Afghans;

e) Since the Taliban proclaims and avows to apply *Sharia* Law, a familiar concept for rural Afghans, to achieve the objective of the creation of just social order, the Taliban is more 'accountable' than the corrupted warlord order, its sole rival in rural Afghanistan. That is, any wrongdoing of the Taliban officials when delivering justice, which means the violation of *Sharia* Law and the principles of *akhlaq*, could be criticized and challenged by people within the context of Islam;

f) The Taliban movement does not represent urbanized elites who have been the occupants of central authority. The Taliban, instead, would be seen as a clear empowerment and imposition of the rural preferred lifestyle over the urban population. The rhetoric of the Taliban, is, therefore, highly enticing for the resilient rural tribal population as a tool to fending off government attempts to penetrate tribal society and a good tool to dominate urbanized elites;

g) The rhetoric of the Taliban is easier and simpler to grasp for the rural people than the rhetoric of the CF-supported central government. While the rhetoric of the central government, which includes alien and complex concepts such as democracy, justice through formal legal codes, the governance of the state institutions, is highly complex and intricate for rural Afghans, and the Taliban's rhetoric, supported with *Quranic* references, would best be defined as 'the struggle of good against evil'. This rhetoric of the everlasting struggle of the good against the evil makes the locals more receptive to the Taliban. 'Why should we fight against the Taliban?' I wonder that how a government official or a CF soldier answers this question to the locals and if the references he/she cites in this answer are simple and clear enough to persuade.

Mainly because of the reasons stated above, the Taliban's rhetoric of fixing and purifying the superstructure, as an alternative governance model to a highly corrupted warlord order in rural Afghanistan entices many people towards the Taliban.

For instance, imagine that you are a young man in rural Afghanistan, little educated, poor, and oppressed by the corrupted warlord order. The Taliban rhetoric could entice you easily. The Taliban rejects all types of social status within the community but the superiority of *taqwa*; upholds the golden Muslim past, embraces you regardless of your ethnic origin, forbids all forms of corruption for others, but permits some activities you may enjoy such as smuggling, kidnapping or fighting for the sake of *Jihad*, which justifies you to bend (not break) the Islamic principles. This rhetoric not only feeds your soul but also provides sanctuary, security and fills your stomach. Most importantly, this rhetoric provides you with an AK-47 rifle, which the traditional religious networks have never done. With this rhetoric in your mind and soul, and the AK-47 in your hands, having once been oppressively ruled, you are ready to seize the political power from the corrupted warlords and government officials. The Taliban offers glory, fame and an opportunity to live a 'meaningful' life for you. That is why, the Taliban finds many recruits among young tribesmen from rural Afghanistan. David Kilcullen identifies this 'pathology' as 'accidental guerilla syndrome'. The 'accidental guerillas' are the neutral civilians who fight alongside the extremists not solely for 'the ideology', but also because they are motivated to fight to protect the existing way of life, or for financial rewards, or for personal grievances.[44] The biographic book, *My Life With the Taliban*, from Abdul Salam Zaeef, who served as the ambassador of the Taliban government to Pakistan at the time of the 9/11 attacks and later sent to Guantanamo, explicitly provides full insight of the motivations and aspirations of a young boy raised in rural Afghanistan.[45] Zaeef vibrantly describes the anarchy and chaos in Southeastern Afghanistan in the early 1980s where local commanders were setting up check points, killing and kidnapping people for money, raping women and promoting lawlessness and vice to the society. Zaeef, as a poor village boy from Kandahar, the son of an Imam who suffers deprivation, develops intense loyalties with his brothers in arms, or the Talibs, and survives in this period of calamity by joining to the Taliban. His utmost aim is to bring justice to the corrupted order by mainly means of trust to his Taliban brothers, his AK-47 in his hand, and the high cause in his mind.[46]

Or, imagine that you are a young woman in rural Afghanistan. Your father, who has to obey the corrupted warlord, promised that you will marry and be the third wife of a wealthy and powerful landowner in the system. You have three options; to commit suicide, to reject this marriage and be killed by your closest relative (preferably your

---

44   David Kilcullen, *The Accidental Guerilla: Fighting Small Wars in the Midst of a Big One* (London: Hurst, 2009), pp.30-32.
45   Abdul Salam Zaeef, *My life With the Taliban* (Melbourne: Scribe Publications, 2010).
46   Ibid, p.20.

brother), or to obey the order. Interestingly, some newcomers, who have been promising to rule with the uncorrupted and just principles of Islam, argue that the marriage could only be carried out with the consent of the first two wives. Unless the husband can obtain the consent of the first two wives, the marriage should not be conducted.[47] Which argument would you support? It is also worth noting that in the post-Soviet invasion period, Qandahar, the province in which prolonged fighting led to a chronic anarchy manifested in rape and abduction of women, was a good example of the turmoil caused by Mujahideen commanders who had become virtual warlords.[48]

Or, imagine that you are a village leader, in whose village there is a need for clean water. You are going to the representative of the warlord to notify him of the urgent problem. This representative asks for a bribe since he personally takes the risk of informing the warlord about the problem and persuading him to resolve it. You do not have enough money to pay the bribe, which is very common practice in contemporary TRMEs. In contrast, Islam forbids every forms of bribe. Some newcomers, who have been promising to rule with the uncorrupted and just principles of Islam, argue that offering and accepting bribes are one of the greatest sins in Islam, and anybody who commits this sin will be severely punished in the governing system they propose. Whom would you support?

Or, you are a religious leader highly revered by the locals in a TRME in rural Afghanistan. You think that the primary reason for the current corruption and carelessness of the warlords toward their followers is excessive modernization and exogenous inputs that spoil the superstructure. The only remedy to fix these deviations is to re-construct the golden age of Islam, which comprises the purist, the most glorious and the simplest practices of Islam. Which course of action would you follow?

Imagine that you are a village leader, or *malik*, in rural Afghanistan. You have the ability to conduct direct communication with the people in the village and persuade them to do, or not to do, or stop doing something if necessary. Likewise, you are the target of the great game between the CF and the Taliban in the current turmoil in rural Afghanistan since you have an absolute authority to conduct negotiations with the representatives of the outside world on behalf of your fellow villagers. You have to be very pragmatic for the survival of your village and security of your people and should know how to play politics to satisfy each player, whether from the outside world or real world. You have to smile temporarily to each party visiting your village even if you do not like them, and show your hospitality. Some of the foreign visitors, who usually cover their eyes with sunglasses, make you suspicious since eyes are the most important organs in your culture when communicating because they do not lie

---

47 See the eye-opening article of Noah Feldman from Harvard School of Law published in *The New York Times* on 16 March 2008. In 'Does Shariah Mean the Rule of Law?' the author explains what Shariah means. <http://www.nytimes.com/2008/03/16/news/16iht-16shariaht.11119704.html?pagewanted=1&_r=1> (accessed 7 September 2009).
48 Barnett R. Rubin, *The Fragmentation of Afghanistan* (London: Yale University Press, 2002), p.xii.

and reflect the real intentions of the heart. These visitors try to win your *heart and mind*, and you know that your heart and mind is not for sale. They have already been reserved by the superstructure since you were born and your utmost aim is to live up those principles.

Nevertheless, you rent your heart and mind to anybody, who pays satisfactorily, so as to guarantee your village's survival. David Kilcullen stresses this very basic instinct of 'survival' prevalent in TRMEs by stating that:

> This is true meaning of the phrase 'hearts and minds', which comprises two separate components. 'Hearts' means persuading people their best interests are served by your success; 'minds' means convincing them that you can protect them and that resisting you is pointless. Note that neither concept has to do with whether people like you. Calculated self-interest, not emotion, is what counts.[49]

For you, as a village leader, is the Taliban a player in the real world or a player from the outside world? Put differently, are the members of the Taliban your sons and nephews who have rebelled against the corrupted tribal order in your region and are fighting for the tribal order? Or is the Taliban a totally alien phenomenon and you have to pretend to support these outsiders with cursed ideas temporarily since they are armed and you have no power to resist?

Your people in the village ask for three things: justice (albeit swift), security and free access to essential services such as clean water, electricity, education and health care. As a village leader, since you do not understand what the state means, from whom would you ask for these necessary services? Surely, you would ask your *Khans*, the executive power in the real world, which had already been providing those types of basic services for centuries. But, unfortunately, the contemporary warlords, who seem to forget their traditional responsibilities to take care of followers and have been involved in the corruption circles around them, do not provide those services satisfactorily anymore. Most of them left you behind and fled to the big cities. In addition, dealing with them under the current circumstances involves you in the corruption. You don't want to be exploited anymore. You just want security, justice and basic services for your village.

What about those people from Kabul, who come to your village once, maybe two times in a month, and talk about the existence of a state – whatever that is? But you hear stories about the piles of cash from Afghanistan that make their way to Dubai every day.[50] You also know that you should pay a bribe for virtually all services you ask

---

49   David Kilcullen, 'Twenty-Eight articles: Fundamentals of Company-Level Counterinsurgency', *Military Review* (May- June 2006), pp.105-107.
50   Michael O'Hanlon, 'Staying Power: The US Mission in Afghanistan Beyond 2011', *Foreign Affairs* (October-December 2010), pp.63-79.

from Kabul's officials, who bought their positions as the highest bidder.[51] What about, then, the foreigners accompanying Kabul's men? These wealthy foreigners that look like *cows to be milked* financially but could they provide security and justice 24/7? Their timid behavior and humorous efforts to leave the village as soon as possible contradict what they are saying. To what extent could you trust them when you ask their help to provide those services 24/7?

What about Taliban newcomers? They argue that they are fighting for the rejuvenation of the structure, to purify it from contemporary earthly sins. Whereas you do not fully agree with most of their practices, the Taliban can provide you and your village with security and justice regardless of your ethnic and tribal affiliation since they recognize and vow to defend your Islamic identity as the primary one. More importantly, if you obey their rules, most of which are the ones that you have already been practicing in your village, then you and your small village can live under their security net. The promise of the Taliban, in fact, perfectly fits for your rural lifestyle. It would also be highly enticing for you as a tool to fending off government attempts to penetrate and intervene in your village. *Who cares about the rest of Afghanistan?* You are only in charge of your village and your utmost objective is to survive. Likewise, since the superstructure orders rulers to be just and merciful, and also provide basic services for the *teb'a* (the society being ruled), you may find a chance to criticize those newcomers religiously if they do not live up to what they offer while they are governing. Additionally, the universally accepted rules of Islam, which ban any type of corruption, the killing of innocents, stealing from the public, torturing indiscriminately and many other sins currently prevalent around you, would guarantee your village's survival since the Taliban, the lesser evil who promise to institutionalize Islamic rule, would deliver enough space for your village to survive as long as you obey.

As a village leader in rural Afghanistan, which part would you prefer to support, or at least pretend to be in favor of? The Taliban or the alliance of the CF-supported central government and corrupted warlord order?

Conclusion

TRMEs in Afghanistan, which constitute perfect cases of societies stuck between extremism and deviants forms of modernism for three decades, would be defined as strictly closed social systems. The turbulent contemporary history of Afghanistan may be broken down into the following periods; Soviet Invasion (1979-1989), Afghan Civil War (1989- 1994), Taliban reign (1994- 2001), and lastly the entrance of the CF (2001-2010). The turmoil we witness today in rural Afghanistan is a direct result of exogenous inputs which have flowed in these periods and weakened the social equilibrium of rural Afghanistan. When these periods are examined meticulously, one may easily notice to what extent rural Afghanistan has been exposed to the bombardment

51   Ibid.

of exogenous inputs. These inputs have primarily caused four profound impacts in rural Afghanistan:

a) The disruption of the traditional socio-political structures and the removal of the traditional tribal elites from the governance in rural Afghanistan, which created a sort of chaotic gap in the executive branch;
b) The emergence of new networks of political Islamists under the flag of the Taliban with the rhetoric of Islamic governance, which, in fact, has redesigned the traditional roles of religious class and has decisively, reconstructed the existing balance of power in rural Afghanistan;
c) Violence has turned out to be a sort of core 'norm' to settle all socio-political and economic issues in rural Afghanistan. Mainly because of the rise of violence as the core norm around which all values are defined, non-violent and pacifist norms, and once were prevalent in the society and rooted from the moral authority that has declined;
d) Traditional economic structures have been completely destroyed, creating space for the resurgence of non-traditional ways of making money such as milking foreigners, warlordism, participating local criminal networks, robbery, kidnapping, and the drugs/arms trade, etc.

3

The Other Side of the COIN in Afghanistan

> Go and love first, then come to me and I will show you the way.
> Hakim Jami of Herat (1414-1492)

This chapter addresses some vital issues on current Counterinsurgency (COIN) strategies in Afghanistan generally unknown by the general audience – yet highly relevant to the end state in rural Afghanistan.

Traditional wisdom defines an 'insurgency' as an important part of unconventional war, or a form of 'irregular conflict' which aims at the overthrow of a constituted government through the use of subversion and armed conflict.[1] Stated another way, an insurgency is an organized, protracted politico-military struggle designed to weaken the control and legitimacy of an established government, occupying power, or other political authority while increasing insurgent control.[2] Political power is assumed to be the central issue in insurgencies; therefore, each side aims to get the people to accept its governance or authority as legitimate. Hence, insurgents aim to break the ties between the people and the government and endeavor to establish credibility for their movement.[3] Put simply, traditional wisdom in the COIN literature defines insurgency as an armed political competition between the government and insurgents over the control of the local population.

It should also be stressed that, in an insurgency, the local population may be categorized primarily into three groups. First are the voluntary insurgents, second are the persuaded or coerced supporters and third are the innocent fence-sitters. Insurgency may start with active support of few enabling individuals, but without passive acquiescence of coerced supporters and innocent fence-sitters, which constitute a majority of

---

1   *FM 3-24*, p.1.
2   *US Government Counterinsurgency Guide*, 'US Government Interagency Counterinsurgency Initiative' (January 2009), p.6.
3   Ibid, pp.1-13.

the population, it is highly unlikely to sustain it. David Galula, a French officer who gained his practical experience in the Algerian War, notes that:

> In any situation, whatever the cause, there will be an active minority for the cause, a neutral majority, and an active minority against the cause. The technique of power consists in relying on the favorable minority in order to rally the neutral majority and to neutralize or eliminate the hostile minority.[4]

In the same vein, John A. Nagl asserts that the obligatory division of 'people from the insurgents' is the chief strategy among the effective COIN strategies.[5] Though distinguishing between these groups with an accurate analysis may be a fundamental task directly linked to the end state in an insurgency, it is the most difficult one since insurgents tend to camouflage themselves among the civilian population. Nevertheless, an effective COIN strategy requires that a COIN force distinguish individuals presenting a threat from innocent civilians. Only after the accurate assessment of the fundamental characteristics coerced/persuaded supporters and fence-sitters such as their ratio among the populace, the demographic and socio-physiological facts of the environment in which they reside, can a COIN force determine the fundamentals of an effective strategy.

The utmost objective of insurgents is to gain control of contested population through a political strategy, which combines persuasive, subversive and coercive techniques, while implementing guerilla warfare to deny the control of the governing authority (a governing authority in TRMEs may not only be the central government but also be a COIN force-supported warlord or tribal leader) over the population.[6] Insurgents apply persuasive techniques, which not only include the promotion of insurgent ideology but also can include the provision of money, access to basic services, control of land and the position for authority. Propaganda is the 'force multiplier' of persuasion, which is designed to control the population's actions, disgrace the COIN forces' actions, provoke the overreaction of the Security Forces and aggravate ethnic, tribal, religious, and sectarian differences.[7] With subversive techniques, insurgents may not only effect the perception of local populace over the COIN forces and the governing authority, but also may exploit the competing power structures in local politics such as tribal leaders, other politico-religious fractions and criminal networks. Lastly, with coercive techniques such as terror, assassination and kidnapping, insurgents would not only intimidate the supporters of the COIN forces and governing authority, but also be

---

4 David Galula, *Counterinsurgency Warfare: Theory and Practice*, (Westport, Connecticut: Preager Security International), p.53.
5 John A. Nagl, *Learning to Eat Soup with a Knife: Counterinsurgency Lessons from Malaya and Vietnam* (Chicago: University of Chicago Press, 2005), p.249.
6 *US State Department*, 'Counterinsurgency Guide' (January 2009). Full document: <http://www.state.gov/documents/organization/119629.pdf> (accessed 12 October 2010).
7 Ibid, p.9.

able to force the local populace to side with them in the conflict. In a nutshell, to gain the support of the local populace (or at least their acquiescence),[8] insurgents follow a protracted low-intensity conflict, which would lead to the exhaustion of the governing authority to break its will. The main effort of insurgents is not to kill as many COIN soldiers as possible, but rather to establish an alternative control over the population.

To fight against an insurgency, there may possibly be two primary approaches. The first one is the enemy-centric or direct approach, the utmost aim of which is to destroy the will of the insurgents to fight by neutralizing their capabilities both in the recruitment phase and in the fighting, or put simply this is 'the approach of killing mosquitoes'. In this kinetically-based approach, COIN forces use attrition warfare and focus their efforts, or all killing power, on annihilating the insurgents by killing or capturing them. In fact, the idea of an enemy-centric approach came from Clausewitz, one of the leading military strategists of modern times. The enemy-centric approach, which he described in his famous book, *On War*,[9] has been facilitated as the primary doctrine by modern armies, and eventually it has been the foundation of military strategy, force structuring, and training for decades. This Clausewitzian doctrine has therefore turned out to be the core principle, around which modern armies are built. Because traditional wisdom considers insurgency a deviant form of war, traditional COIN strategies and doctrines are based on the same notion as the more general approach to war. When the conventional direct approach is applied to the COIN, therefore, the focal assumption is that COIN forces should find and isolate insurgents first, and then focus its killing power on the insurgent's decisive point. In David Killcullen's words, this approach could be summarized with the motto 'first defeat the enemy, and all else will follow'.[10] Furthermore, following the Clausewitzian view which postulates that war is essentially and inherently political, traditional wisdom in COINs solely focuses on the political causes and dimensions of insurgency, and tends to omit other dynamics such as socio-cultural and economic ones that may drive an insurgency.

The hot debates on the US military missions in Afghanistan in the fall of 2009, for instance, revitalized the debates on conventional enemy-centric approach. The strategy of reducing the US involvement in the nation-building efforts and ramping up drone attacks and covert raids against high profile al-Qaeda targets in Pakistan's tribal areas, which was first proposed by Vice President Joe Biden, is a perfect case for this approach. *The New York Times* highlighted this strategy, the principal rationale of which was to neutralize al-Qaeda members, by reporting that 'rather than trying to protect the Afghan population from the Taliban, American forces would concentrate on strikes against al-Qaeda cells, primarily in Pakistan, using Special Forces, Predator

---

8   *US State Department*, 'Counterinsurgency Guide' (January 2009).
9   'What is war?', the first chapter 'On War', <http://www.gutenberg.org/files/1946/1946-h/1946-h.htm> (accessed 26 September, 2010).
10 David Kilcullen, 'Twenty Eight Articles: Fundamentals of Company-Level Counterinsurgency', *Small Wars Journal* (March 2006): <http://smallwarsjournal.com/documents/28articles.pdf> (accessed 10 August 2010).

missile attacks, and other surgical tactics.'[11] In the same vein, Ralph Peters writes that the CF forces in Afghanistan should concentrate on the destruction of al-Qaeda and its allies, and nothing else matters in this mess.[12] He continues that:

> Here is a simple way to conceptualize our problem [in Afghanistan]: a pack of murderous gangsters holes up in a fleabag motel. The feds raid the joint, killing or busting most of them. But some deadly ringleaders get away. Should the G-men pursue the kingpins, or hang around to renovate the motel? Common sense says: Go after the gangsters. They are the problem, not the run-down bunkhouse. Yet, in Afghanistan, we've put the bulk of our efforts into turning a vast flophouse into the Four Seasons – instead of focusing ruthlessly on our terrorist enemies. It is politically correct madness.[13]

It also should be noted that since the primary objective of the enemy-centric approach is the physical component of insurgents, and the kinetic capabilities and intelligence efforts of COIN forces carry utmost importance during the planning and the implementation of a COIN strategy.

In conventional terms, when applying the enemy-centric approach, the best military tactic is the search and destroy mission. The search and destroy mission is the tactical offensive method which is employed by ground and aerial military forces in short durations to contact, attack, exploit and pursue the enemy.[14] The utmost aim of this method is to develop a situation to establish a direct fire contact or to regain it with the insurgents. If the precise location of the enemy is not known, the objective of contact would be achieved through patrolling roads and villages with platoon or company-level units, or with sweeping operations in a particular area with units larger than a battalion. If known, the contact would be achieved by launching an attack, the types of which could be a hasty, deliberate or a special purpose. This said, in this method, which directly targets the physical component in an insurgency, the priority of the COIN forces seems to conduct 'kill/capture missions' concentrating on the battalion or brigade-size sweep operations and direct actions carried out by elite forces on the ground, and precision air strikes. The search and destroy missions are not only easier to plan for military staff, but also endow immediate and quantifiable effects which can be followed and measured metrically. For instance, the number of missions or the number of killed/captured insurgents, as adequate statistical data easy to measure, would be good indicators when defining success. Search and destroy missions, therefore, perfectly fit for the conventional military planning and conduct of

---

11   Peter Barker, and Elisabeth Bumiller, 'Obama considers a strategy shift in Afghan War' *The New York Times* (22 September 2010). Full text: <http://www.nytimes.com/2009/09/23/world/asia/23policy.html> (accessed 1 September 2015).
12   Ralph Peters, 'Afghan Agony: More Troops won't help', *New York Post*.
13   Ibid.
14   *FM 3-0*, Department of Army, 'Operations', pp.7-16.

the operation, and thus, for modern armies, there has emerged an institutional inclination to apply this method over time in every campaign they encounter.

After explaining this conventional wisdom in COINs, I should also note that anybody who grabs a hammer will see every problem as a nail. Put another way, would the officer corps and the soldiers, who have been trained or indoctrinated to fight against the enemy with search and destroy missions, assess every incident in their area of responsibility in the COIN theater as a nail to a hammer? Or would they be competent, cross-culturally well-equipped, innovative and longsighted enough to unchain themselves from their institutional indoctrination of appraising each case in the theater through the lenses of this conventional wisdom? The answer to this question, which, in fact, reflects the current dilemma of the tactical and operational level planning in rural Afghanistan, is extremely relevant in determining the end state of the insurgency.

The second primary approach is the population-centric one which mainly targets the coerced supporters and innocent bystanders, and aims to control the population – or put simply, this is 'the approach of draining the swamp'. According to this approach, if the objective of establishing control over the population and the environment in which the people live can be achieved, then the insurgents would be deprived from shelter, supply, recruitment, and more importantly moral legitimacy. Among the followers of this approach, Galula proposes that COINs are not only primarily military conflicts but also a combination of socio-political, economic and military ones. He also suggests four laws in the implementation of an effective COIN strategy. These are:

a) the aim of the war is to gain control of the population rather than control of the territory;
b) most of the population will be natural in conflict; support of the masses can be obtained with the act of active friendly minority;
c) support of the population may be lost. The population should be efficiently protected to allow it to co-operate without fear of retribution by the insurgents;
d) order enforcement should be done progressively, that is, removing insurgents, gaining support of the locals, building infrastructure, and setting a long-term relationship with the local population.[15]

Galula also contends that:

> A victory [in COINs] is not the destruction in a given area of the insurgent's forces and their political organization. A victory is the permanent isolation of the insurgents from the population, isolation not enforced upon the population,

---

15 David Galula, *Counterinsurgency Warfare: Theory and Practice* (Westport, Connecticut: Preager Security International), pp.54-56.

but maintained by and with the population. In conventional warfare, strength is assessed according to military or other tangible criteria such as the number of the divisions, the position they hold, the industrial resources they obtain. In revolutionary warfare, strength must be assessed by the extent of support from the population as measured in terms of political organization at the grass roots. The counterinsurgents reach a position of strength when his power is embedded in a political organization issuing from, and firmly supported by the population.[16]

Similar to Galula, Thomas X. Hammes contends that COIN is a different kind of war, a fourth generation warfare which is centered on the battle of ideas and winning the support of innocent bystanders and coerced supporters, not the physical destruction of the enemy.[17] In the same vein, General David Petraeus explicitly states that 'the decisive terrain is the human terrain. The people are the center of gravity. Only by providing them security and earning their trust and confidence can the Afghan government and ISAF prevail'.[18]

To win the support and legitimacy of the local populace, or to win their hearts and minds, the COIN forces should apply unconventional approaches, which would generally be hard to explain with traditional military wisdom. The term 'hearts' represents the emotive component, which indicates that the victory of the COIN forces will best serve the long-term interests of the local populace. The term 'minds' represents the cognitive component, which indicates that the COIN forces will win the war eventually, and therefore, to side with the COIN forces would be the better choice for the local populace. According to David Kilcullen, 'neither concept [neither winning hearts nor winning minds] has to do with whether people like you. Calculated self-interest, not emotion is what counts'.[19] Then, one may conclude that winning hearts and minds would, in fact, be an applicable strategy as long as it serves for the interests of population.

To win the hearts and minds of the local populace, the population-centric approach should include:

a) separation of insurgents from the populace;
b) securing the populace against the threats of the insurgents;

---

16 Ibid.
17 Thomas X. Hammes, *The Sling and the Stone: On War in the 21st Century* (St. Paul, Minneapolis: Zenith Press, 2004), p.321.
18 Full text of the Counterinsurgency Guidance of Gen Petraeus (1 August 2010). <http://www.isaf.nato.int/from-the-commander/from-the-commander/comisaf-s-counterinsurgency-guidance.html>
19 David Kilcullen, 'Twenty Eight Articles: Fundamentals of Company-Level Counterinsurgency', *Small Wars Journal* (March 2006): <http://smallwarsjournal.com/documents/28articles.pdf> (accessed 10 August 2010).

c) establishment or strengthening of existing governing institutions to be legitimate in the eyes of the populace;
d) establishment of the rule of law, or a just social order.

Since the utmost objective of the population-centric approach is the psychological component of the local population, an inter-disciplinary understanding should be nurtured through the synthesis of different fields such as political, social and behavioral sciences. Since the population-centric approach targets the value system of the local population to gain their consent, an effective and comprehensive COIN strategy cannot be crafted without referencing to fields such as sociology, psychology, anthropology, economics, and theology. The value system of a society may be defined as a set of socially shared ideas of what is good, right and desirable. With proper mechanisms, it is likely to influence and regulate the value system of the local population in a timely manner. In traditionally slow, complex and fragile societies like the ones in TRMEs, however, to tailor a proper mechanism to regulate the value system of the local people at an appropriate rate would be a very hard and extremely slow process. Nonetheless, the population-centric approach assesses that it is worth trying. This slow process of regulating the value system in TRMEs, however, may be less likely to serve the needs of a COIN force with less commitment and strategic patience and with not enough time.

Furthermore, the population-centric approach possesses an inherent challenge for COIN forces – namely, both COIN forces and insurgents aim to de-legitimize the authority of other of the population. The de-legitimizing phase gives advantages to insurgents since COIN forces must destroy insurgents or deny their access to the local populace in order to maintain legitimacy, whereas insurgents only need to 'survive' to undermine the perceived control of the COIN forces over population. If so, insurgents may win the war by just not losing it.

Unlike the enemy-centric search and destroy missions, the clear-hold-build method places the support of the population as the core of all efforts, and therefore is used as the primary tactical method for the population-centric approach. This inherently defensive method includes removing insurgents from an area with military force and by force if necessary, and then securing the area and defending it from the attacks, and lastly establishing permanent governing institutions – host nation government in a conventional sense – to create a stable and secure environment.[20] By applying the 'clear' phase as the first stage, a terrain base is aimed to serve subsequently as a staging point for future operations and the expansion of the control of the COIN forces. Authority and security could be achieved and strengthened as long as the COIN forces stay in that particular terrain in the 'hold' phase. When that particular terrain is determined to be independently functioning, the COIN forces would implement

20 *FM 3-24*.

the 'build' phase, with stability initiatives, including enhanced security, services and development.

One should note that population-centric approach does not mean that COIN is less violent than the enemy-centric one. The *US State Department's Counterinsurgency Guides* explicitly writes that:

> It [the population-centric approach] is an extremely difficult undertaking, is often highly controversial politically, involves a series of ambiguous events that are extremely difficult to interpret, and often requires vastly more resources and time than initially anticipated. In particular, governments that embark upon COIN campaigns often severely underestimate the requirement for a very long-duration, relatively high-cost commitment (in terms of financial costs, political capital, military resources and human life).[21]

It also continues that:

> A purely enemy-centric approach might work against incipient insurgencies that are led or centrally controlled by a particularly charismatic or powerful individual. However, historical experience has shown that against mature insurgencies and complex, non-hierarchical insurgencies, population-centric approaches have a higher likelihood of success.[22]

In reality, a sound COIN strategy would seldom be purely population-centric or enemy-centric, but, by and large, would be a combination of both, with a relative balance changing over time, area and the strategy of insurgents. Nonetheless, these approaches function as the starting points when crafting an effective COIN strategy. Which one would be the foundational principle or initial point when tailoring a COIN strategy specifically designed for the TRMEs?

First of all, fully relying on my field experience in the TRMEs of five different states, I embrace the population-centric approach as the primary route which would lead us to the end of the tunnel. During the literature review, I, interestingly, notice that roughly all individuals who have hard-earned field experience are in favor of engagement with the populace to gain their support as the core of any COIN strategy in Afghanistan. In contrast to their conceptualization of the population-centric approach, the ones who sit in their air-conditioned offices and who do not smell the soil of the COIN environment, are inclined to focus on an enemy-centric approach and tend to disregard the importance of the legitimacy of the population. This difference would, in fact, reflect the fundamental debate on how to address the current insurgency in Afghanistan. Following the dictums of the facts on the ground, should

---

21 *US State Department*, 'Counterinsurgency Guide' (January 2009), p.12.
22 *US State Department*, 'Counterinsurgency Guide' (January 2009), p.15.

we pursue a risky population-centric strategy, which will surely necessitate long-term commitment and strategic patience? Or should we answer to the emergency calls of strategic exhaustion, and solely go after al-Qaeda and the Taliban members, which would be a less risky – thanks to the drones – strategy that does not call for long-term commitment? Stated another way, should we attempt to drain the swamp and take the risk of being choked while doing this, or should we cheer and be satisfied by only killing one or two mosquitoes at a time?

I wholeheartedly contend that we should drain the swamp with accurate strategies, because everybody in the outdoor business knows that it is merely impossible to fight against mosquitoes by killing them one by one.

First of all, I would clearly suggest that the argument of 'every insurgency is local and village/district level COIN strategies must be applied to dissolve the current insurgency in rural Afghanistan' is theoretically true. For Coalition Forces in rural Afghanistan, the objective of reaching to the village/district leaders and to get their full support for COIN seems to be the first and foremost objective since they, as the intra-tribe leaders, are the ones with the unique ability to shape the ideas and behaviors of the people they are in charge of. It is probable to assert that without reaching to the village/district leaders it is impossible to suppress the insurgency in rural Afghanistan. Nonetheless, before answering the questions of what are the fallacies COIN strategies currently applied in rural Afghanistan and 'how' to suppress the insurgency, here are some points for the strategists.

First, I assume that the people in rural Afghanistan do not have the notion of central authority, or the state, and the state is not a viable player in their real world. So the premise of traditional wisdom that emphasizes the government-based strategy is futile when crafting a COIN strategy in rural Afghanistan.

Are the Coalition Forces a legitimate player in the world of rural people in Afghanistan, or an agent of the outside world? The CF is likely to be a player of the outside world since traditionally there have been two legitimate players in the real world in rural Afghanistan: tribal leaders at the seat of the executive, and religious leaders at the seats of the judiciary and legislation. How do we demarcate the borders of the real world in rural Afghanistan? Any place where the people shape their ideas and practices in accordance with the superstructure is the real world. Since it legitimizes itself by avowing to abide by the superstructure and even disseminating the Islamic rhetoric of *purifying the corrupted tribal order and evicting the foreigner supporters of the corruption*, the Taliban can operate without difficulty in the real world, which means the Taliban has the privilege to contact with the intra-tribe leaders, and even with the individuals at the bottom. By being able to reach every individual (bottom-to-top approach), the Taliban is not only able put extra political pressure on the village/district leaders to influence their political preferences, but also able to create alternative political space so as to replace the traditional village/district leaders to govern that particular village/district, as they did against many tribal leaders.

On the other hand, the CF, as a player from the outside world, has been doomed to apply a top-to-bottom approach to reach to the village/district leaders. For this

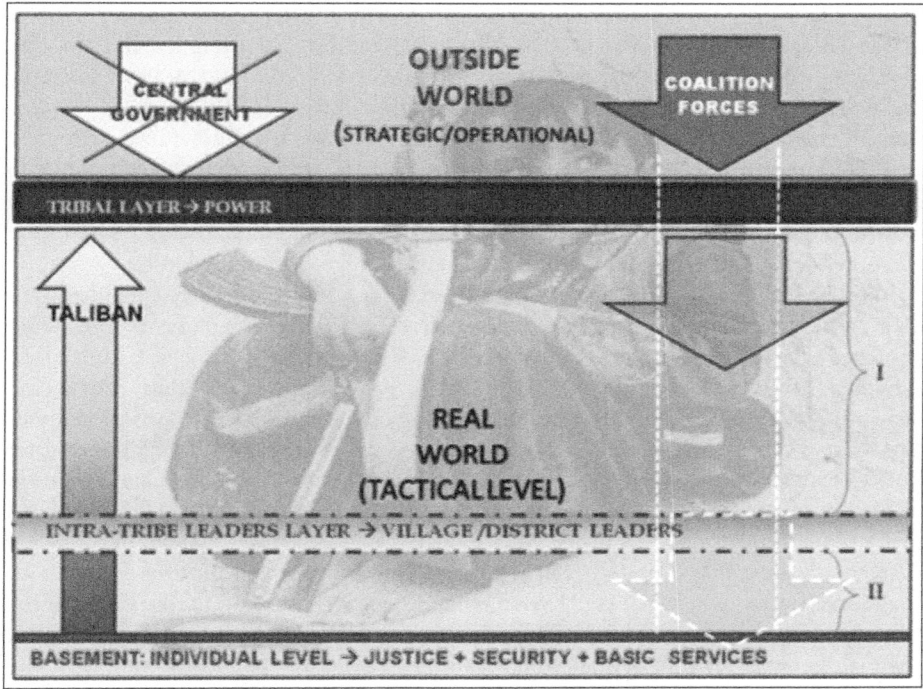

Figure 2 A chart portraying rural Afghanistan.

reason, it is impossible for the CF to employ long-term strategies in the real world of rural Afghanistan since it is doomed to be absent from the legitimization of the superstructure. More importantly, even in their attempts to reach to the village/district level – let alone individual level – which means that the CF should breach the tribal layer that constitutes the border between the outside world and the real world, CF encounter strong opposition of the tribal leaders. In the light of the fact that it is a must for the CF to operate on the village/district level, there are two possibilities. The CF can try to penetrate into the real world of rural Afghanistan with the consent of the warlords, whose sole aim is to seek more political and military power, or without their consent. If the CF decides to operate with the consent of the warlords and give them what they want, the CF would then be adding more corruption to the system, the first dynamic which alienates people in rural Afghanistan. If the CF decides to penetrate into district/village level without consent of the corrupted tribal order, then this penetration is an immediate threat for the corrupted tribal order. This dilemma, which the CF is currently experiencing in rural Afghanistan, turns it into a passive player, rather like 'a cow to be milked' by the locals in the real world.

What about sparking religiously motivated insurgency, as a bottom-to-top approach, which worked so well against the Soviets during their invasion in Afghanistan, to shatter this highly corrupted and hard to penetrate tribal layer so as to freely operate in the village/district, maybe even in the individual level? Unfortunately, the seat of Islamic insurgency against the corrupted tribal order has already been filled by the Taliban. Put ironically, the CF in rural Afghanistan would look up for inspiration or down in desperation but not laterally for 'co-operation' since the extremely corrupted contemporary tribal order and the Taliban, two mutants which claim to be representative of the superstructure, are equally dangerous for the CF. It is also worth mentioning the symbiotic relationship of these mutants, namely as long as the corrupted tribal order lasts, the Taliban finds enough ground to exploit it.

Let's assume that you are a company commander who has recently been deployed to a rural theater in Southeastern Afghanistan with your company. Before being deployed, you have read all available pieces on COINs including David Galula, T.E. Lawrence, Robert Thompson, David Kilcullen, John Nagl, and Ralph Peters. You have studied *FM 3-24* and all other available manuals to broaden your vision about this kind of conflict to get familiar with. You have made all necessary reading to better understand the history of Afghanistan. You also have studied the roots and evolution of extremist movements in Islam such as *Salafi/Wahhabi* thinking. You have watched many movies to get plugged in the situation such as *'Black Hawk Down'*, *'The Battle of Algiers'*, *'The Last Samurai'*, and even *'Avatar'* to better understand how to engage with the locals. Lastly, you have been given a comprehensive orientation program from the leaving company commander and been briefed about the primary local dynamics of the insurgency after your arrival. Thanks to the orientation, you know all locals who to trust and not to trust, you have got acquainted with your local web of intelligence, and more importantly you have inherited a good 'archive' of your predecessors from the leaving company commander to be used as a reliable source when crafting your own local COIN strategy. You have been warned that 'the intent of the commander' is blurred and there have been no clearly set military objectives to achieve at the tactical level. In this cloudy world, you have concluded that 'innovation' and 'initiative' are the most risky words, which would not only distract the COIN strategy of your area of responsibility already settled by your predecessors but also would endanger the lives of your soldiers. Therefore, to strictly stick to the 'archive', or to follow the footsteps of the previous commanders, is the best way when faced with a problem. If things went wrong it would be the archive to be blamed, not you.

The rotation has been completed and the company from which you have taken the responsibility has left the theater. You have been in charge for almost a week. You are informed that a group of local leaders came for a welcome visit. Though you have visited these leaders during the orientation with the leaving commander, this will be your first direct contact with the local leaders since taking the command, which means that this will be your first challenge. You know from the archive that they have been the most reliable and co-operative partners in your area. You also know that your predecessors worked closely with them and they have been the principal local constitutes of already settled COIN strategy in your area. Besides, you aware that they are the ones who will solve all your problems. They are the ones who run the local market from which your soldiers go shopping. They are the ones who work as local contractors in your area, who provide water, transportation, construction assistance and many more things that is directly related to the comfort of your company. Put simply, they are your 'legs and arms' in this hostile region full of 'bad guys'. That is why you, as an astute commander who knows that the first impression is the last impression in TRMEs, endeavor to impress them, or 'win their hearts and minds'. You have sent one of your soldiers to accompany them to your office, and in the meantime, you have reviewed every piece of information about COINs in your mind.

You are ready for your first challenge. They are in your office. You welcome them with very shiny words out of your office and accompany them into your office. As a cross-culturally competent leader you stand until the last guest seats and prefer to seat with them, not to your official seat behind the desk. They insist you to seat your official seat, but you kindly reject this proposal by saying that you do not like any obstacle between you and the locals such as the desk, and you always want to be among them. You also remark that you do not want to hide yourself behind the desk, as you always favor openness and sincerity among close friends. What a cool start!

After an exchange of greeting words, one of the elders in the guest group says through the interpreter:

> First, we came here to help you in your fight against the insurgents. We are the local leaders who fought with your predecessors against the bad guys in this area. We have been defending our people with your help against the threat of the insurgents at all costs, and thus helping you as local supporters. We are on your side and your most trusted partners. During this fight with the insurgents, my son was killed, my nephew was severely wounded, and my niece was kidnapped. Many in the group have also paid the price of siding with you by seeing the deaths of their beloved ones like me (agitation phase). This is a brutal fight and our fight with the bad guys is a matter of life and death. This fight turned out to be personal 'vengeance' for most of us (the stress of determination). We are here today to thank for your support in our fight with these bad guys. We are very eager to fight with them, but we have some issues you should know from the first day (the main theme is coming).
>
> During our fight we do not want you to see and hear everything. There would be some 'nasty' issues you would see/hear around. Some people may complain about our handling of the fight to you. But this is a tough fight as you know and we should be very aggressive enough to meet the challenge posed by the insurgents. This is a nasty fight which forces us to follow nasty rules. Be assured that we are always on your side (building of trust). But what we are doing in this area is not only for the safety of the local people but also for your safety (covert threat).

You carefully listen to the sayings of the elder and take notes to look 'engaged' in what he wanted to say. Though you cannot fully grasp what the elder is trying to say mainly due to the poor translation of the interpreter and the indirect messages given in the speech of the elder, but you nod him several times and clearly show your confirmation. To try to decode the ciphers of indirect messages of a speech spoken in a foreign language and received through an incompetent interpreter, what a mess! This very first meeting with the local leaders finishes and you presumably cannot decide whether it went well or not. As the commander in charge, though you need time to figure out what 'normality' means in this area, and this 'early' meeting and the things your guests try to express raise a lot of question marks in your mind.

Over time, you have come to realize what 'nasty issues' brought up by the elder in the first meeting means. You realize that the elder who puzzled you in the meeting is the leader of the local drug network, the other elder in the group runs the local smuggling business. Two of them are trying to seize the fertile fields of poor villagers. One of them illegally controls the local water resources. One has ties with corrupted government officials and embezzles the money sent from central government. One is in charge of a tribe, which has been in a kind of feud with another tribe and tries to align with you to dominate the rival tribe. One controls the local market and created a sort of monopoly to be able to easily rip the locals off. But all have been fighting with COIN forces against the insurgency. Welcome to the real world of insurgency. You realized that the tendency to categorize each player in your local theater as 'a friend' or 'an enemy' is wrong. There is purely no 'black' or 'white' in TRMEs; instead there are gray tones. Many of your local allies fighting against insurgency may seem to be the bad guys bullying and exploiting the local population. What do you think: are they 'bad guys' or 'good guys' for you as the local representative of the COIN forces? This is your first dilemma to address. That is, will you try to stop them bullying the local population, which means that you will intervene in the local politics or will you omit these 'nasty' issues of local politics and evaluate them with their performance in the fight against the insurgency? You have been indoctrinated that your utmost aim is to protect the local population in a COIN environment. Will this principal rule in the COIN literature be valid in this case? If you decide to protect the local population from these guys, will you be strong enough to bear the consequences of breaking 'the hearts and minds' of your 'local allies in the insurgency?' Does protecting locals from the criminal acts of your allies mean risking your soldiers' lives? Put simply, which one would be true: to play an active role in the local politics at the expense of alienating your old allies in the insurgency, or playing 'three monkeys' (don't listen, don't see and don't speak) when it comes to the local politics to be solely able to focus on your sole objective: fighting the insurgency?

At first glance, you may think that this scenario is only fiction and the locals who fight with the COIN forces in an insurgency – the locals for instance in Afghanistan – are the 'angels without sin' who solely try to rescue local population from evil insurgents. Based on my field experience, I should stress that this is a general pattern, which, more or less, has been experienced by every tactical level leaders who fight against the insurgencies of Afghanistan and Iraq. Following our company commander example, how would you decide: to dive into the matters of local politics to protect the population even from the misbehaviors of your allies, or to play 'three monkeys' to focus on the insurgents and not to risk the lives of your men? If you chose the first option and craft your COIN strategy accordingly, the first reaction of this 'corruption circle around you' will be to visit you for the second time. In this second 'unfriendly' visit, they will warn you that these 'nasty issues', have been addressed in their first visit and you have confirmed their handling of the insurgency. Saying nothing to them meant saying 'yes' for them. They will try to explain that being in silence in the first meeting is confirming what they have said and your interference to their business is the denial of what you have talked in the first meeting. They also re-emphasize their covert threat: 'but what we are doing in this area is not only for the safety of the locals but also for your safety', however this time openly. How would you react to this open challenge? Would you dare to follow what you believe in or retreat with political maneuvers? Please remember that your answer to this question will be directly linked to these three things: the end state of the insurgency in your area of responsibility, security of the local population, and security of your soldiers. I am sure that you will find the right answer as the company commander.

I should also stress that well-respected leaders in your area of responsibility, who can play a bridge role for you to access to the 'silent majority', never visit you. Since you are the local representative of one side of the conflict as the COIN commander, these fence-sitter bridge leaders never support you and your cause openly. This said, you should go out, analyze local politics, drill down the fundamentals of it and figure out who assumes the bridge leader roles and how to engage them, but at the expense of losing your 'local good allies' with bad habits. Given that you nailed the identities of the right bridge leaders, whose support can dramatically change the nature of insurgency in favor of CF, then the question I would raise is that if you are determined enough, to contact them by taking the risk of alienating your local allies.

Following this example, I want to outline some other dilemmas which have been faced mainly by the CF forces in the TRMEs of rural Afghanistan. These dilemmas I aim to highlight carry utmost importance for the end state of the insurgency in Afghanistan.

Justice vs. Security: Which one is the core of COIN efforts in TRMEs?

Winning support of the population would often entail a breaking of physical, ideological, financial and more importantly psycho-sociological linkages between insurgents and the population. That is why an appropriate COIN strategy should be designed to exploit potential fracture lines between insurgents and the population. In TRMEs, the most significant line that connects the population to insurgents is the notion of justice and the degree of which the population perceives insurgents as the justice-deliverer. Reminding the notion of justice in TRMEs as the core principle around which all other socio-political and economic phenomena revolve, this section re-emphasizes the importance of justice. It is an undeniable fact that there has been a huge gap in the emerging COIN literature with regards to the impact of the notion of the justice on locals in TRMEs, presumably because justice looks more like a matter in the fields of law, theology and sociology rather than military strategy. COIN strategists may, thus, disregard the notion of justice by claiming that it is not purely military and cannot be integrated into an effective COIN strategy. In contrast, I stress that the notion of justice in TRMEs should be the most significant phenomenon, which determines the end state of the insurgencies in TRMEs. That is why justice, the impact in the TRMEs of which should be analyzed with an interdisciplinary approach, must be studied very meticulously when tailoring an effective COIN strategy.

Let's take the rural Afghanistan as a case. Following our example of the village leader, and as the village leader, people expect you to deliver justice to settle the disputes no matter if they are rooted from social, economic and political affairs. Which authority should you turn to ask for the delivery of the justice to settle the disputes and comfort the sides in it? When you look at the CF to ask for the delivery of the justice, you would notice the 'this is none of our business' attitude and their pointing out the formal legal system and the courts of the central government. What about the courts and formal legal system of the central government? The current government-facilitated justice system is extremely slow, corrupt and insufficient to impose the rule of law in rural Afghanistan. The best offer is to settle the dispute within an uncertain period of time – maybe years later – in favor of the side which pays more. On the other hand, when you turn to the Taliban for the delivery of the justice, the justice system of the Taliban is swift and relatively just, since it takes its legitimacy from the *Sharia* Law – one of the primary sources of the superstructure. Furthermore, you would have a chance to criticize the judgment, if it may seem to violate the tenets of the superstructure. The justice system proposed by the Taliban entices many in rural Afghanistan since:

a) It is delivered by a man on a motorcycle carrying only the *Quran* and a document to record the agreed judgment. It is, therefore, swift, mobile and one call away from the locals;
b) It is compatible with the basic tenets of the superstructure. The judgments are, therefore, more or less 'predictable';
c) It is not a 'one-size-fits all' system; instead, is specifically tailored for that particular area. It is, therefore, highly adaptable to the specific characteristics of that particular village;
d) It is relatively more just and a cleaner system than the legal system of the central government.

At first glance, establishment of security may seem to be the fundamental enabler for the other COIN efforts such as establishing rule of law, to constitute administrative mechanisms and developing judicial activities. COIN forces would, therefore, excessively focus on security when designing a strategy. In TRMEs, however, the question of to which party will the local population turn to for the settlement of disputes carries utmost importance for the future of COIN efforts. I would suggest that if a dispute is perceived to be settled unjustly by the individual exposed, or the settlement delays, this unjust settlement or long delay not only humiliates that individual but also disgraces the reputation of all the family or tribe collectively in TRMEs. In this case, security becomes an irrelevant concept which may be easily underestimated. While justice is a necessary precondition for the establishment of a secure environment in TRMEs, a secure environment does not necessarily provide the just settlement of disputes. The ones who are killed while seeking for justice, for instance, are highly commended by the local community in TRMEs. Success of any COIN strategy in TRMEs is difficult to define since traditional wisdom usually takes into account the level of security as the measurement of success. I strongly suggest that the percentage of the disputes settled by the COIN force-supported governing authority in the total disputes should be the main indicator of the success. To reformulate, the level of perception of locals to see COIN force-supported governing authority as the justice-deliverer should be the measurement of success of the COIN efforts in a particular area.

Strategic Ambiguity: To fight an insurgency with a 'coalition of willing'

As a tactical level commander, I asked or answered this very basic question maybe thousands of times during my military service: 'who is in charge in here?' In military terms, this basic question reflects one of the principles of war, 'unity of command', since unity of command is best achieved by vesting a single commander with requisite authority.[23] Who is in charge of the COIN efforts in Afghanistan? This is a very basic question which is directly linked to the end state of the insurgency. Which is the best answer: the US military or NATO, or United Nations or Kabul, or international non-governmental organizations? The existence of multiple-headed international structures and involvement in a complex form makes the COIN efforts more complicated though not necessarily effective. Hence, how this principle has been forsaken in the evolution of military command for Afghanistan carries utmost importance.

For instance, as of May 2010, the International Security Assistance Force (ISAF) in Afghanistan includes 85,795 troops from 43 different states.[24] Let me reiterate the unprecedented departure from the principle of unity of command in Afghanistan in 2006, when Combined Forces Command-Afghanistan (CFC-A) passed control of the ground fight to the ISAF, and operations became split between several unified or 'supreme' commanders in charge of US Central Command, the North Atlantic Treaty Organization, and US Special Operations Command.

Similarly, in 2006, after the formation of the UN Assistance Mission in Afghanistan (UNAMA), the reform package on security issues was divided into five areas which would be led by a lead-donor nation: the US would be responsible for military reform,

---

23   *US Department of the Army*, 'Field Service Regulations–Operations, Field Manual 100-5', (Washington, DC: US Department of the Army 1954), pp.25-27.
24   <http://www.nato.int/isaf/docu/epub/pdf/placemat.pdf> (accessed 15 November 2010).

Germany for police reform, the UK for counter-narcotics, Italy for judicial reform, and Japan for disarmament, demobilization and reintegration of ex-combatants in Afghanistan. The Provincial Reconstruction Teams (PRTs), which made the CF's expansion to rural areas easier by facilitating reconstruction services, have been formed from the militaries of different states and civilians from NGOs, or UN and NATO officials. There are 172 licensed NGOs from about 40 different states and 60 different international organizations currently operating in Afghanistan.[25] According to the recent Congressional Research Service (CRS) report, as of March 2009, there are 68,197 Department of Defense (DoD) private contractors in Afghanistan; about 9,300 were US citizens, 7,000 third-country nationals, and 52,000 local nationals.[26] Interestingly, the CRS report continues that private contractors made up 57 percent of the Pentagon's Afghanistan personnel and concludes that 'this apparently [represents] the highest recorded percentage of contractors used by DoD in any conflict in the history of the United States'.[27]

Seeing that the security situation has been getting worse since 2006, the US wants to share the burden of fighting the insurgency with other NATO members and coalition partners. That is why NATO has increasing roles and activities in Afghanistan, but there has still been no clear consensus among the allies over what role NATO should play in Afghanistan and which responsibilities it should assume within the ISAF mandate. The differences among allies concerning NATO responsibilities has led to a 'coalition of willing' type of support within NATO. Each state that formed the coalition willingly sends their troops to the field in Afghanistan, stipulates the roles and extent of their contribution as well as under which circumstances they take responsibility. As of 22 December 2009, the Afghan National Army (ANA) has an actual strength of approximately 130,000 personnel, but plenty of caution against placing too much emphasis on units of the ANA rated as 'capable' that have yet to prove themselves in the field.[28]

In a nutshell, who will hunt down the insurgents, or trace opium producers, or fight against corruption, provide justice and security, help reconstruction, disarm/demobilize/reintegrate ex-combatants, implement development projects, train Afghans, fulfill peacemaking/peacekeeping missions, conduct humanitarian relief efforts, make political and socio-economic reforms etc. is up to the coalition of willing members comprising the COIN front in Afghanistan. Nonetheless, it is sad to see that there is no 'unity' in the contents or scale of the responsibilities that the military and civilian members of the COIN front take within the scope of comprehensive and cohesive

---

25   For full information on NGOs operating in Afghanistan: <http://afghanistan-analyst.org/ngo.aspx> (accessed 16 November 2010).
26   Full report: <http://www.fas.org/sgp/crs/natsec/R40764.pdf> (accessed 16 November 2010).
27   Ibid.
28   Jeff Haynes, 'Transition to ANA must start now', *Defense News* (19 July 2010): <http://www.defensenews.com/story.php?i=4716194> (accessed 16 November 2010).

COIN strategy in Afghanistan. This fatal deficiency shows the high need to develop a coordinated institutional capable coalition that is willing to continue to focus its attention on dealing with COIN efforts in Afghanistan. Put differently, the answer to the question of who is to be blamed for the failure of COIN in Afghanistan or to be praised for the success of it has still been unclear.

CF as a 'Cow to be Milked' in Rural Afghanistan

This is one of the most challenging dilemmas faced by the CF in rural Afghanistan. In any prolonged fight conducted by wealthy armies such as the CF against any insurgency in a socio-economically deprived and highly isolated environment such as rural Afghanistan, there emerges a very simple question: who is the real exploiter of the continuation of the insurgency? That is, conventional COIN strategies focus on the political landscape of the environment and place the political rivalry at the epicenter of the insurgency. This inclination to overemphasize on the political phenomena in COINs may cover the financial struggle of the locals. Any soldier of a wealthy army in impoverished environments is not only a highly valuable target for the insurgents, but also highly valuable asset in economic terms for the locals. To reformulate the question stated above, who is the real exploiter of the continuation of the insurgency in economic terms?

Let's take a brigade-level unit with 2,000 soldiers locked in a container-like and cloistered base in Afghanistan. Assuming that the lines of logistic support are perfect, the soldiers of this brigade still want to spend money since shopping is a social phenomenon which comforts people in times of stress. If each soldier spends averagely $200 in a month for eating local foods, buying souvenirs, and for other needs during his/her deployment, totally it makes $400,000 cash flow to the local markets monthly. Let's add sub-contractors, who conduct small business for the brigade and assume that they earn $100,000 monthly, and add the payments of the intelligence community of that brigade for the valuable tips to the informers and corroborators and assume that they earn $30,000 monthly. Let's add the gifts given to the local community leaders in the area of the responsibility of that brigade to make them happy and comfortable and assume that they cost $20,000 monthly. Additionally, let's add the equipment and gear given to the locals to be used during the operations or trainings, the ending point of which is the local black market, and assume that they cost $10,000 monthly.

Presumably, as the biggest economic enterprise in that particular area, the total contribution of this brigade to the local economy is nearly $550,000 monthly. The brigade, the official mission of which is to bring security in its area of responsibility, is likely to be seen as a factory, which spreads wealth and employment and boosts the local economy. In a society, like the one in rural Afghanistan, which is still dominantly on the first level of Maslow's motivational pyramid and has been trying to use every means to survive, a single dollar would mean a good cause for the people to fight.

Who benefits from this spread of wealth? If the answer is the same sub-contractors, the same interpreters, the same traders, the same market owners, then it means that there is a big problem. Any clever soldier in this kind of environment is inclined to maintain the interactions with the recommended or familiar individuals for security reasons. The routine procedure is to work with the most trusted locals recommended by the predecessor. At first glance, this is the best solution since security is the top priority. Nonetheless, day by day, month by month, year by year, unintentionally, this procedure leads to the formation of a thick 'corruption circle' around the soldiers. For the soldiers, this is not a corruption since this security measure probably saves lives. However, when we look at the other side of the coin, from the perspective of the locals, this is the *corruption* which let the *selected ones* to be benefited from the spread of wealth coming from our factory, the brigade.

In a typical TRME, the locals want either *less corruption*, or *more chance to participate in it*. For the people in rural Afghanistan, the rhetoric of *less corruption* is more likely to be represented by the Taliban, and the rhetoric of *more chance to participate in it* is more likely to be represented by the corrupted warlords and government officials, who benefit by aligning with the CF. The violence, at least in the local level, will turn out to be a fierce and brutal fighting between the happy minority, who have benefited from the economic and political privileges of being the trusted ones of the CF, and the desperate majority who want nothing but for the *equal share of corruption* flowing from the CF. Consequently, it is likely that every passing year makes the corruption circles surrounding the bases of the CF forces thicker, and after passing a certain threshold, it is impossible to decide who is exploiting whom and for what purposes. Who are the real enemy and the ally in the insurgency, a 'happy minority' who enjoys the privileges of milking the CF exuberantly, or the 'frustrated majority' who cannot access the CF to milk? If one additional personnel of the CF means a 'drop' to the pool of the corruption, then what should be done is to economize the numbers of personnel in the theater and maximize their efficiency.

In TRMEs, being illiterate does not necessarily mean being an idiot. The locals in TRMEs, who have seen many rotations of COIN forces, have known their strength and weakness, and more importantly their organizational vulnerabilities in military, financial, socio-cultural and political terms. That is why the 'happy minority' who enjoy milking the international efforts of TRMEs is primarily motivated by pragmatic considerations and very good at exploiting the coordination deficiencies of the international efforts. For instance, the local labor market would be a good indicator of how perfectly the locals exploit the job opportunities bestowed by different international institutions/organizations in that particular area. A driver of a non-governmental organization may, for instance, be employed as an interpreter overnight by Special Forces units, which pay more; or a local, who has been trained as a police by the CF forces in Afghanistan, my find a profitable position in a private security company. This was the case, for instance, for our efforts in Kazakhstan in 2003. Though we trained roughly 300 personnel for the Kazakh Army and established the first elite unit of Kazakhstan, KAZBAT-A Battalion, I was shocked to hear from one of our students two years later, that roughly 80 percent of that personnel resigned from the military and got very profitable positions in private security companies easily with the certificates delivered by us.

Another important example of the 'cow to be milked syndrome' of the COIN forces is the local intelligence market. The desperate need of COIN forces to acquire local intelligence and a bountiful budget of intelligence-gathering business creates a profitable market for the 'happy minority'. In the many theaters I have served in so far, I witnessed that the local intelligence market constitutes one of the best functioning markets which promote the local economy. Its opaque nature and inherently existing rule of compartmentation promotes the participation of the locals to this market and being a well-paid informer of the COIN forces would be a good second job for many locals. Over time, the 'invisible hands' of the market regulates the prices of each type of intelligence tip and everybody in the market gets to know the exact price of each type of intelligence tip. Even some in the market may sell tips both to the COIN forces and insurgents to maximize their profit. Interestingly, I witnessed in Iraq that the insurgents and locals cooperated in the intelligence market to milk the COIN forces. It was an interesting experience to see how smart the local insurgent cell was to finance itself from the COIN forces by only selling tips to the COIN informers about their activities. That is, while the exact price of an AK-47 in the local arm market was $100, we learnt that simply by buying four or five of them and paying $400-500 in total, the local insurgent cell sold the intelligence tip of a weapon cache to the COIN forces via double-informers to the price of $1,000.

Local Politics vs. Insurgency: Whose hands are in whose pocket?

At the strategic level, there are three players in the insurgency: insurgents and counter-insurgents as the active players, and local populace as the passive player. 'Insurgency' may simply be defined as a prolonged political rivalry between these two active players for the decisive victory of achieving the political support of the local population. By and large, the news on any insurgency is served by the media to the international audience at the strategic level mainly due to the need of simplifying the incidents in the insurgency as a play with three players. For instance, the Western audience reads news about the insurgency in Afghanistan beginning with the titles, in which these three players are generally the objects or subjects. Many still think that insurgency is a sort of armed competition between good guys and bad guys for the support of the neutral majority. They also are inclined to categorize each individual as a 'friend' or 'foe'. This inclination of oversimplifying the incidents into a game with three players in the insurgency – and the habit of getting rid of every detail – may lead to unintended consequences (the primary of which is the underestimation of all other dynamics in the game). 'All other dynamics' of a particular incident in any insurgency should, in fact, be analyzed by tactical-level leaders such as platoon and company commanders. Only tactical-level leaders, who have been cross-culturally competent and have plugged in to the local environment, could analyze 'the details' and decode 'the local ciphers' of that specific incident. The process of decoding the local ciphers of each incident is, in fact, directly linked to the success of the COIN in that particular area.

Let's assume that an Improvised Explosive Device (IED) attack in which three CF soldiers are killed has recently happened in the X province of Y district in rural Afghanistan. The Western audience reads or watches this attack with these titles: 'three CF soldiers have been killed in a Taliban IED attack in Afghanistan' or 'insurgents killed three CF soldiers in Afghanistan' or 'an IED attack has claimed the lives of three CF soldiers in Afghanistan'. This attack, which could be summarized and simplified into a sentence at the strategic level, may, in fact, mean days of investigation and hundreds of pages for an astute and competent tactical leader, who aims to decode the local ciphers with a systemic approach. For instance, an IED attack cannot be carried out without the efforts of leaders, financiers, suppliers, recruiters, trainers and foot soldiers of the insurgency in that Y district. An accurate analysis of the attack should start with the correct interpretation of the aspirations and motivations of each of these constituents of the attack. It is highly unlikely to assert that all these actors in the IED attack act solely with ideological reasons. In the light of the 'cow to be milked syndrome' of the wealthy COIN forces in the impoverished insurgency environment, the involvement of some would be primarily from economic reasons. The anger of an ex-contractor of the COIN forces, whose contract has recently been declined, would be a much more prevailing motivation for him than the concept of global *Jihad*; or the personal grievance of an individual, whose relatives have recently been killed in a drone attack and have been labeled as 'collateral damage', could be a more powerful motive for him to join this band; or this attack may be carried out with the full consent and support of a tribe as a move against the rival tribe in a feud; or this attack may be planned by a local warlord to get his local opponent messed with by the CF; or the location of this attack could be chosen by the elders of the village, which aim to get the CF forces concentrated on by the rival village. Put simply, economic, socio-political, psychological motives or interests of individuals or groups such as tribes, villages, local political factions and warlords may blend with the ideological motives in this IED attack. In a nutshell, there could be involvement of different aspirations and motivations in this IED attack, which the Westerners read or watch in the news as the act of insurgents solely carried out by ideological reasons. Relying on my field experience, I would explicitly contend that in roughly all attacks I encountered, different motives and aspirations of individuals and groups intermingled with the ideological motives. I captured an ex-contractor, whose water-carrying contract had been declined, as the placer of the IED in a road to our battalion. I captured a villager whose livestock had been killed accidentally by our forces, as an informer who reported the movements of our troops. I witnessed the exploitation of our forces by the tribal leaders who sought for more power against their rival tribes. I came across many times that to what extent the economic struggle between the 'happy minority', who exuberantly milk the COIN forces, and the 'frustrated majority', who seek for the equal share of the corruption flowing from the COIN forces, shaped the fundamental dynamics of the insurgency. I witnessed the misuse of our troops in a water dispute between two villages. I witnessed how a fight between rival tribes over pastures shaped the local politics in that particular area. I encountered how the marriage problem of a husband and wife from different tribes led to local inter-tribe feud and predominantly shifted the political stances of the players in the insurgency. Put differently, I have witnessed many times: water or land disputes, an honor killing, a marriage, a young lady, an economic transaction between two individuals, a decline of the contract, an inter-tribe or intra-tribe rivalry, a leader struggle in a tribe, a rivalry between different religious sects, a rivalry between different local political groups, and how personal grievance shaped the local politics – and consequently the nature of insurgency – in that particular area. Following our IED example, an IED attack which claimed the lives of three CF soldiers would mean a water or a land dispute, an intra-tribe/intra-family feud, or a decline of the contract. Even a marriage problem may be the primary reason of the exact location and timing of the IED attack, or even the attack itself.

In conclusion, I wholeheartedly suggest that, all Afghan politics in rural areas is local, and in many incidents at the local level, COIN forces are the subject of the game rather than being the object. I have witnessed many times that it was the local politics that drove the insurgency. It was the actors of the local politics that shaped the environment and aptly made use of the fight between the insurgents and COIN forces. Therefore, an accurate analysis of who is exploiting whom and for what purposes carries utmost importance when addressing an incident concerning the insurgency. In the many theaters I have served so far, the rivalry has been among the actors in the local politics, and the COIN forces, or outsiders, were merely pioneers in their local chess game. Being fully aware of the complexity of a multitude of identities, communities, socio-political, economic and religious networks in a particular geographic proximity in rural Afghanistan, I would suggest that the interactions of the locals who live in that proximity shape the local politics, and local politics dominates the insurgency. In many incidents, the fight has been, thus, among the actors in the local politics, which means that it was not a fight between the insurgents and the COIN forces as we read and watch in the media. Nonetheless, I have great concerns if the CF forces currently have astute, cross-culturally competent and well trained tactical-level leaders who could easily understand how local politics shape the nature and future of insurgency.

The Dilemma of Strategic Inputs and Tactical Outcomes

I have been trying to follow every report made public for almost two years in the US regarding COIN efforts in rural Afghanistan. The point is that roughly all reports which have been written to date are addressing the strategic level, or to some extent operational. They present strategic recommendations or suggest strategic approaches to resolve the current dilemma in Afghanistan. This means that roughly all current literature on Afghanistan aims to address the strategic inputs. How many soldiers do we need in Afghanistan? How much money should we invest? Which kind of resources do we need? Which sort of strategy should the Obama Administration craft? On the other hand, we have to recognize this fact. The current war in rural Afghanistan is a rural and local one which has been conducted in harsh weather and terrain conditions and against extremely devout believers. This is a tactical fight which you can only fight with a 'boots on the ground' strategy. David Galula writes that:

> The basic unit of counterinsurgency warfare is the largest unit whose leader is in direct and continuous contact with the population. This is the most important unit in counterinsurgency operations, the level where most of the practical problems arise, where the war is won or lost.[29]

As a person in the business of execution, and as a military man who participated in many COIN operations at the tactical level, I would surely contend that the 'organizational capacity' of the CF at the tactical level in Afghanistan is less than the required level to win the war. Interestingly, nobody currently discusses this phenomenon in the US, and the US military also do not mention this deficiency. You may invest billions of dollars and send thousands of soldiers to the area of theater, but what about the *outcome* of these efforts at the tactical level? Believe me that as a person who knows this business and has seen many things with my own eyes, I surely contend that the outcome of all these efforts at the tactical level cannot win the war in Afghanistan. Currently, some in the US are meaninglessly discussing the strategic issues. Nonetheless, neither President Obama nor General Petraeus, but the 'organizational capacity of the CF soldiers at the tactical level' will win or lose the war. Put simply, the billions of dollars and thousands of soldiers about to be sent to Afghanistan, as strategic inputs have little impact on changing the course of the war unless they serve to promote the tactical effectiveness and efficiency. In fact, all of the resources that the US and NATO are contributing to Afghanistan – the tens of thousands of soldiers and the billions of dollars – may only be the steps of a strategic solution to a tactical problem. Until CF redirects its tactical efforts towards the TRMEs, these new resources will be naught due to the level of analysis conflict. There should be fostered more accurately analyzed mechanisms to transform the efforts at the strategic level into 'effective' tactical outcomes.

I should also stress that, most recently, the conceptualization of contemporary insurgencies has been broadened to the widest level through the inclusion of the term 'global insurgency led by al-Qaeda-like transnational networks'. This is a very assertive term used to define insurgencies in a contemporary security environment that supersedes the national level and has global reach, and has influenced beyond domestic borders of Afghanistan – hence, the conceptualization of a global insurgency that distracted the needed focal focus on COIN efforts at the tactical level in local areas in rural Afghanistan. In this context, the existence of external factors such as al-Qaeda

---

29   David Galula, *Counterinsurgency Warfare*, p.32.

elements and their involvement in the insurgency in Afghanistan constitute an obstacle to focus on tactical level when crafting COIN strategies in rural Afghanistan. This obstacle makes the insurgency in rural Afghanistan, which in fact is a simple fight that should be addressed with tactical-level efforts to gain the optimum consent of local population, unnecessarily 'complicated' when conceptualizing the insurgency in rural Afghanistan. Assessing the insurgency in rural Afghanistan as a fraction of the global insurgency, thus, may lead the military planners to think it more as a matter of enemy-centric strategic planning and less as a matter of population-centric tactical planning, which in fact has been the real remedy for the rural Afghanistan. Interestingly, when talking about Afghanistan, I observed from a great majority of junior-level officers from the coalition countries such as the US, Germany, Canada, and Poland that they are inclined to explain their presence in Afghanistan by claiming that Afghanistan is currently the most important front against global insurgency. Many of them think that their presence in Afghanistan and fighting the global extremism in the soil of Afghanistan is a wiser option rather than fighting extremism in Washington DC, Berlin, Ottowa, and Warsaw. Then, they come with the explanation that they are in Afghanistan to protect their countries from global extremism, which means that Afghanistan is simply a front in this grand struggle and Afghans are 'unlucky residents' who happened to be born in this important front. This motivation to be used to explain their presence in Afghanistan, dangerously, may not only 'dehumanize' the nature of COIN efforts but also may lead to the fatal mistake of regarding Afghans as 'the collateral damages' of this global insurgency. As long as there emerges no threat to the residents of coalition countries, it may not be a big trouble to see dying Afghans. It would not be exaggerated to assert that the end state of this motivation is a pure enemy-centric approach, which takes no notice of the local populace.

'Hi-Tech Trap'

It is true that kinetic hi-tech capabilities constitute a principal method to break the will of insurgency to continue the struggle whether a COIN force embraces a population-centric or an enemy-centric approach. Currently, the CF in Afghanistan, however, has been experiencing a sort of 'hi-tech trap', which has fallen by the technologically advanced armies fighting in the 'primitive' terrains such as rural Afghanistan. That is to say, this is an 'uncomplicated war' which must be conducted by simple foot soldiers (boots on the ground strategy), with the simplest means and procedures. If the numbers of the COIN soldiers who are watching the war from their screens are more than the numbers of soldiers who see the pupils of the insurgents with their own eyes, COINs cannot disrupt this insurgency. Stated another way, the more soldiers you have fighting the insurgency from behind their screens in their hi-tech bubbles, instead of fighting on the ground in the theater of war, the more easily you fall into this trap. If COIN soldiers are not able to see, smell, taste, and, more importantly, feel the theater (by saying 'feel the theater' I mean to fully understand the terrain and weather conditions, and the agonies, perceptions, motivations, hatred, and happiness of the local people who live in it) they experience a sort of alienation from the reality on the ground. Mainly due this deficiency, the CF fall into the nirvana fallacy of 'capability-based planning'. I define 'capability-based planning', one of the most strategic mistakes currently made by the CF, as desperately relying on the highly sophisticated hi-tech weapon systems such as unmanned aerial vehicles, aircrafts, surveillance radars, attack helicopters and making plans considering these 'capabilities' first without thinking about the necessary imperatives of COIN. For instance, suppose that there is a suspicious meeting of a so-called Taliban commander in a village. Who gave this intelligence tip? Was it a local collaborator? May this tip be confirmed and is the source reliable or not? But the point is since the commander sitting in the op-center is *capable* of destroying that house with a sudden air raid without taking the risk of sending troops to this village, it is likely that he is more inclined to prefer an air raid as a low-risk solution rather sending troops to the village. It is these hi-tech assets which could deceivably and overwhelmingly make the commanders 'capable' to react to anything suspicious in his area of responsibility without considering the extent of reliability of the target and unintended consequences such as the notion of collateral damage. Currently, however, the CF forces in Afghanistan have ample kinetic capabilities/resources to conduct direct military attacks but inherently are limited by the availability of the legitimate targets.

These hi-tech kinetic capabilities 'dehumanize' the nature of the fighting for the commanders, which must be fought as a human-centric COIN. I should also note that the term we use – 'collateral damage' (a phenomenon mainly rooted from the excessive reliance on the hi-tech kinetic capabilities – is the 'sons, daughters, mothers and fathers' of many in TRMEs.

The recently available video of a 2007 helicopter attack in Baghdad by the US military – WikiLeaks-published footage showing the political effects (which is likely to rival the Abu Ghraib prison photos as a source of Muslim outrage)[30]- would be a grim example.[31] In this bloody attack, 12 civilians were killed, including a Reuters photographer and his driver. Here is an example of the 'hi-tech trap' in which modern armies keep their soldiers at a safe distance from the insurgency they are fighting.

They start to live a virtual reality. They fight as if they are playing a video game and become brutal and reckless. The senseless and shocking words of the pilots in the footage will really hit anybody to watch. They sound like they are sharing a video game rather than a real-life battle in which they are killing civilians. This footage will as well be remembered as a good example on how to make a strategic mistake for the sake of tactical accomplishment.

30 Elisabeth Bumiller, 'Video Shows US Killing of Reuters Employees', *The New York Times* (5 April 2010).
31 Footage: <http://www.huffingtonpost.com/2010/04/06/wikileaks-iraq-killing-vi_n_527383.html> (accessed 6 October 2010).

I should also underline that while the CF in rural Afghanistan has the 'capability' to destroy a village within 10 seconds with hi-tech capabilities, it has no 'capacity' to hold this village 24/7. On the contrary, by sending two foot soldiers with AK-47s in their hands and a high cause in their mind, the Taliban has the capacity to hold this village 24/7. The CF, with all resources and hi-tech weapon systems, though *capable* to do anything in seconds, has no *capacity* to project the presence 24/7 in rural Afghanistan. This fact turns the CF into an 'unreliable and weak' player in the eyes of rural people. In contrast, the Taliban though technologically weak and with limited capability, has the *capacity* to project the presence 24/7 in rural Afghanistan, which makes it more reliable and a strong player in the game. In an insurgency, the side which is able to establish 24/7 presence in residential areas outruns the other. The objective of establishing 24/7 presence could only be achieved by living in close proximity to the population, rather than raiding in to the residential areas from remote and isolated operational bases.

Nirvana Fallacy of Force Protection: Trying to feel the environment behind the bullet-proof glasses and cloistered bases

In the *FM 3-0* Manual of the Army, force protection is defined as a package of measures:

> ... to prevent or mitigate hostile actions against DoD personnel, resources, facilities, and critical information. These actions conserve the force's fighting potential so it can be applied at the decisive time and place and incorporates the coordinated and synchronized offensive and defensive measures to enable the effective employment of joint force while degrading opportunities for the enemy...[32]

The CF force has built Forward Operation Bases (FOBs) across Afghanistan to provide security for the soldiers and, launch and support tactical operations. Large FOBs, in which thousands of soldiers could stay, offer all comforts that can be found in any Western city such as coffee shops, restaurants, massage parlors, shopping malls, well-equipped gyms and movie theaters.

Graeme Wood writes that in Afghanistan, some soldiers are pampered and continues:

> ... being on a big military base can feel a bit like being on a cruise ship. Grand exertions are made ensure comfort, and leisure is organized: basketball at six, bingo at 11. B-list celebrities, armed with camera-ready smiles, are on the deck

---

32   *FM 3-0*, 'Operations'.

to shake your hand. To keep the coalition forces happy, starting point is food. The food is rich and plentiful...[33]

He then adds that the restaurants in Kandahar Airfield, with prestigious examples from North American, Mediterranean, French and Dutch cuisines, are scattered among 'a vast array of tents – mostly half-pipe structures with wooden interiors and air-conditioning'.[34]

FOBs highly require personnel to function and to secure. Hundreds of the soldiers could be assigned for the task of securing FOBs instead of contributing to the overall COIN efforts. Furthermore, when significant resources are diverted to support the FOBs which are supposed to support operations, then we may assert that there is a problem. The problem is fourfold. First, is that to observe the life from the cloistered FOBs may isolate the CF forces from the Afghan population. The boundary of FOBs may not only be physical but also a physiological and cultural one, which divides soldiers 'on the one side, the people whose trust, safety, and information they should be securing on the other'.[35] Second, excessive emphasis on the force protection, the heart of military doctrine of the US military in conventional terms, may be seen as proof for the locals, whom the CF should protect, that the CF looks like it cannot even protect itself. Third, the FOBs, which can easily be monitored 24/7 by the insurgents, make the CF 'predictable' in every movement, and therefore increase the vulnerability of the soldiers. Fourth, the FOBs, which function as the anchors for soldiers who are reluctant to sacrifice their luxury way of life, turn the operations in to routine, limited, and short duration patrolling missions in the proximity of them.

A large number of CF troops have been concentrated in Kabul, Kandahar and other big cities of Afghanistan, roughly 80 percent of which is rural. Thousands of US soldiers are stationed at Bagram Air Base, shopping centers of which are highly popular among CF soldiers. Bagram Air Base is located hundreds of miles away from the insurgency. On the other hand, the contact of the CF soldiers in rural areas where the Taliban control, is rare, timid and limited to daylight hours. The Taliban seem to be highly aware of the fact that the center of gravity in the fight in Afghanistan is the rural areas, where the CF are seldom seen.

Highly Visible Foreign Presence in Afghanistan: A part of a solution or a problem?

Specifically in TRMEs, the legitimacy of foreign presence in the eyes of the locals is a crucial component of a successful COIN. Accordingly, in the case of TRMEs of Afghanistan, where a strong 'skepticism' towards the presence of foreigners – in

33 Graeme Wood, 'An Air-Conditioned Nightmare', *The Atlantic* (August 2008).
34 Ibid.
35 Norman Emery, 'Information Operations in Iraq', *Military Review* (May-June 2004).

particular foreign military forces – exists, it is essential to establish some form of legitimacy in rural Afghanistan. With a highly visible, large-scale and long-term ground presence, however – which is currently the case in Afghanistan – it is highly unlikely to establish legitimacy. The term 'occupation', as the misadventure in Iraq has clearly demonstrated as well, has the disastrous effect of giving extremists a powerful recruiting tool that they are quick to exploit and a good propaganda theme to effectively disseminate. A night letter sent from the Taliban to the locals siding with the CF says that:

> Muslim Brothers: understand that the person who helps launch an attack with infidels is no longer a member of [the] Muslim community. Therefore, punishment of those who cooperate with infidels is the same as the [punishment of] infidels themselves. You should not cooperate in any way -neither with words, or with money, nor with your efforts. *Watch out not to exchange your honor and courage for power and dollar.*[36]

According to many in the Muslim world, 'the US-led coalition's very presence in Afghanistan fuels an indigenous insurgency. It keeps the flame of transnational terror alive and blocks the return of Afghan refugees to their villages'.[37]

Then it is likely to assert that the presence of non-Muslims in this almost exclusively Muslim land of rural Afghanistan constitutes a powerful tool for the rhetoric of extremists. When I interacted with the locals in Afghanistan as a Muslim soldier, I witnessed that many describe the US-led coalition as 'crusaders' and are inclined to equate it with previous invaders such as the British and Russians. Furthermore, sensitivity to the non-Muslim military presence in their homeland bestows the Taliban-led Afghan insurgent's common cause with global transnational extremist networks such as al-Qaeda. Put differently, the foreign military presence originates a 'solidarity among Muslim brothers' and constitutes a fundamental reason for the cooperation of the local insurgents most of whom even cannot accurately show the location of the US in the world map and global extremists who seek for proper grounds to challenge 'infidels' militarily. Foreign military presence functions as a good bridge to combine local considerations with global aspirations. Stated another way, foreign presence is the most important obstacle before the divorce of the marriage of 'local considerations rooted mainly from Pashtun nationalism and religious reflexes, and 'global extremism'.

On the other hand, one should note that the immediate withdrawal of the CF from Afghanistan is not the solution. Nevertheless, to keep the presence and visibility of the CF in every COIN effort 'low profile', to increase the visibility of Afghans, and to

---

36 Human Rights Watch, 'Lessons in Terror': <http//www.hrw.org/campaigns/Afghanistan/2006/education/index.htm> (accessed 14 November 2010).
37 Arif Rafiq, 'A Muslim Solution for Afghanistan', *Christian Science Monitor* (6 October 2009).

increase the number of Muslim troops in the CF may be the proper solutions for now to neutralize the very basic propaganda theme of the extremists.

Insurgency takes patience: Insurgency is not something to learn in a four to six-month deployment

My shortest deployment was three months long and I gave two years of my life for the longest one. I was sent to four and six month-long deployments as well. In the light of this experience, I suggest with full confidence that it takes almost the first three months for a tactical leader to adapt to the new environment mentally and, at least, to reach a preliminary analysis about the local politics, insurgency and their relation with one another. The last two months, on the other hand, are, by and large, reserved for packing 'the stuff'. This process of packing 'the stuff' does not include physical activities regarding the departure such as shopping for souvenirs, and preparing the archive for the upcoming successor, but also includes a mental and emotive component. Any tactical leader, who has been excessively bombarded with thousands of issues, needs to reset his memory. His/her motivation and performance, thus, declines and he/she experiences a sort of alienation from the environment.

Put simply, it takes three months to adapt to the local environment and the last two months are reserved for packing 'the stuff'. Then I should suggest that the most efficient performance of a tactical leader is the period between the first three months and the last two months. Any deployment shorter than five months means confused and cloudy leaders at the tactical level roaming around without clear and sharp focus on the insurgency and local politics.

Going Tribal and Buying Security

When the incompetency of the central government to stabilize rural Afghanistan was understood, military strategists, who have sought for new options to target the Taliban and al-Qaeda fractions, the feasibility of recruiting Afghan tribesmen has increasingly been a hotly-debated issue among the US government, academia and think-tank community. This strategy of going tribal has gained ground specifically when the strategy of building '*Sunni* awakening councils' against insurgents in Iraq emerged as a success story in 2006. Simply, copying *Sunni* awakening councils and pasting them to rural Afghanistan would be a success story as well.[38] For instance, in his interview in *The New York Times*, General David Petraeus emphasized the thickening of 'local forces as well, through greater political engagement of tribes and reconciliation with

---

38 Greg Bruno, 'A Tribal Strategy in Afghanistan', *Council on Foreign Relations Publication*, (7 November 2008). Full report: <http://www.cfr.org/publication/17686/tribal_strategy_for_afghanistan.html_> (accessed 17 October 2010).

fighters who were not hardcore'.³⁹ He continues that 'certainly many on the ground think that perhaps in certain areas local reconciliation initiatives hold some potential'. He was right about the experiences of US soldiers who managed to feel the realities on the ground. By mainly means of some soldiers in the US military, who served in Afghanistan and came to realize the importance of tribal dynamics and the incompetence of state-centric approaches in rural Afghanistan with their own eyes, there has recently emerged a vast literature about the strategy of countering insurgency at the local level.⁴⁰ A local initiative of tribal structures may be the first line of defense against the insurgents in the countryside. In the same vein, during a speech at the US Institute for Peace in Washington, Defense Secretary Robert Gates acknowledged his support of bringing supra-national elements into the fold by stating that 'at the end of the day, the only solution in Afghanistan is to work with the tribes and provincial leaders in terms of trying to create a backlash against the Taliban', yet he recognized that he did not know 'how this strategy would evolve'.⁴¹ How would this strategy evolve? The answer of this question does, in fact, mainly rely on how the CF implements this strategy. When established literature of going with supra-national elements in rural Afghanistan is reviewed, it is evident that many studies in this literature, though they correctly diagnosed the current turmoil in rural Afghanistan, have proposed excessively inaccurate strategies such as going tribal and buying security from the tribal structures as their prescriptions. Though the authors of these studies spent some time in TRMEs and closely experienced the importance of supra-national dynamics in rural Afghanistan, they are, fatally, inclined to measure power in material terms in TRMEs. Major Jim Gant, for instance, states in his report 'One Tribe at a Time' that 'Money and guns equal the ultimate power' in TRMEs. He continues that 'power in this area [in TRMEs] was about the ability to put armed men on the ground to attack an adversary or to defend the tribe. Guns were the ultimate currency'.⁴² As a 'hard-head' Special Forces soldier, his argument could be seen accurate at first glance. I, however, contend that the power rooted from the 'money and gun' strategy could foster temporary solutions on particular issues in specific part of TRMEs, but cannot cultivate a stable, permanent and comprehensive end state. The end state of the reliance of material powers to mobilize tribes against a common enemy is warlordism –

---

39   Carlotta Gall, 'Insurgents in Afghanistan Are Gaining, Patreous says', (30 September 2008). Full interview: <http://www.nytimes.com/2008/10/01/world/asia/01petraeus.html> (accessed 24 October 2010).
40   Jim Gant from US Special Forces, 'One Tribe at a Time'. Full report: <http://rohrabacher.house.gov/UploadedFiles/one_tribe_at_a_time.pdf> (accessed 17 August 2010). David S. Clukey from the US Air Force, 'A District Approach to Countering Afghanistan Insurgency', *Naval Postgraduate School Thesis*: <http://edocs.nps.edu/npspubs/scholarly/theses/2009/Dec/09Dec_Clukey.pdf>. Papers delivered in Tribal Engagement Workshop of the *Small Wars Journal* (25 March 2010) <http://smallwarsjournal.com/events/tew/>
41   Greg Bruno, 'A Tribal Strategy in Afghanistan'.
42   Ibid.

the symbiotic relationship of which with the Taliban, in fact, feeds the current chaos in Afghanistan. Any strategy, the reference point of which is not the superstructure, is null and void.

Engagement should be based on the objective of reaching to all power sources in a geographic area, which I will refer to as 'community engagement'. Solely engaging specifically selected tribal leaders could subvert non-tribal sources of power.

The engagement strategy should not be solely built on particular tribes or individuals, since engaging only selected tribes and individuals could alienate other tribes and power brokers in the local politics such as religious and socio-economic networks in the same geographic area. Any money which goes to one particular individual or one particular interest group in TRMEs may be called a contribution to the local corruption and warlordism. In November 2009, Hanif Atmar, the Afghan Interior Minister, said in an interview that a few militia commanders, who were specifically selected and supported with the Local Defense Initiative of the CF, in the Northern city of Kunduz, turned out to be local warlords after they acquired power (money and arms) from the CF. He also adds that after expelling the Taliban, they started collecting taxes from the locals.[43] That is why, after seeing that the Local Defense Initiative fostered decentralization and local chiefdoms, US Ambassador Eikenberry temporarily suspended it out of the fear that it was creating a new breed of warlords.[44]

'I can beat you with my primitiveness!'

In the summer of 2003, I was the leader of a liaison team in Iraq to accompany a group of local fighters during an operation. We came together with the leaders of the local fighters for a last coordination meeting at the nightfall. After the completion of the coordination meeting, which, in fact, increased the numbers of questions in my mind mainly due to the poor translation and differences between me and the local commander on how to conduct the operation, I started to harness my gears to get ready for the operation. First, I checked my pistol and my rifle, and then my thermal camera mounted on the rifle, radios (one for my unit and one for local commander), GPS and so forth. During this last check, I saw two local fighters staring at me with a sarcastic smile in their faces. Both were wearing old sandal slippers with soft rubber on their feet, and carrying old AK-47s. The one, who was carrying a watermelon in a plastic bag, asked while smiling 'hey bro, are you flying to the moon?' I could not understand what he intended to say and asked. He said 'you are like a very hi-tech man in a space mission; this will be a simple operation, no need to get panicked'. I came to realize, then, that as a modern soldier harnessed with the gear which worth more than $50,000, how naïve I was before these two fellows, a total cost of whose stuff was roughly equal to the cost of my GPS. I also came to conclude that the notion

---

43   Henriksen, 'Afghanistan, COIN and Indirect Approach', p.68.
44   Ibid.

of courage is twofold. One is courage rooted from the knowledge, in which a highly trained and well-equipped modern soldier tries to follow. He aims to know everything in the theater to lessen the risks involved in the mission. He cautiously steps forward and endeavors to take well-calculated risks with maximum knowledge. The other one, in contrast, is courage rooted from illiteracy and fatalistic mentality. This 'ones who think their end cannot be heroes' mentality excessively ungrounded the sense of pride and the ability to sustain physical stress coming from the harsh terrain and weather features (when blended with religious motives) unconventionally and asymmetrically turn a tribesman wearing rubber slippers and carrying a watermelon in a risky operation into a warrior perfectly fit for the unique conditions of TRMEs.

Fully recognizing the motto of 'I can beat you with my primitiveness!', which fits in rural insurgencies with tough terrain and weather features, I would raise the question of whether or not the CF forces are adequately equipped – both in material and psychological terms – to fight 24/7 under the physical and mental/emotive conditions dictated by the *primitive lifestyle* in rural Afghanistan?

At the tactical level, for instance, marriage of a typical contemporary soldier and his motorized vehicle dictates that the soldier remains close to his motorized vehicle and to the equipment which was designed to be carried by the vehicle. However, the current conflict in rural Afghanistan is a light-infantryman's war. During the Soviet invasion, the Soviet ground forces developed the *bronegruppa* concept[45] to use the firepower of their personnel carriers in an independent reserve once the motorized rifle soldiers had dismounted. However, terrain in rural Afghanistan often dictated that vehicles could not follow or support their squads. This concept gave the commander limited maneuverable reserve since the soldier was never supposed to be more than 300 meters – the range of an AK-47 – from his vehicle. Thus, at the tactical level, the question of whether the CF in rural Afghanistan is capable of divorcing from their motorized vehicle to catch up the insurgents, and the length of this divorce – both in terms of distance and time – is highly correlated with the efficiency of the COIN forces at the tactical level in rural Afghanistan.

---

45 With this concept the Soviet ground forces could attack independently on the flanks, block expected enemy routes of withdrawal, serve as a mobile fire platform to reinforce elements in contact and serve as a battle taxi to pick up forces. Yet, since dismounted Soviet soldiers were less agile and heavier than a typical Afghan fighter, they could not catch up with them. This was the main reason that lay behind the ineffectiveness of the *bronegruppa* concept. Nonetheless, for many Soviet strategists, even to be able to conduct dismounted operations within the 300 meters' range of the carriers was a revolutionary change in their doctrines when thinking of the harsh terrain conditions of rural Afghanistan: Oleg Kulakov, 'Lessons Learned From the Soviet Intervention in Afghanistan', (Roma, NATO Defense College: Research paper No. 26, March 2006). Also: <http://fmso.leavenworth.army.mil/products.htm#conflictaf> (accessed 8 July 2009).

Interpreters: Cordial friends or pragmatists?

Based on my field experience in Iraq, Afghanistan and Central Asia, to fight with an insurgency where you speak the language and an insurgency where you do not speak the language are totally different things. The ability to interact directly with the locals, consequently, is closely related to the end state of the insurgency in that particular area. In an insurgency where we cannot speak the native language, we have the sole option of using the interpreter for making us be understood properly by the locals. We may either use a non-resident interpreter or a local one. Local ones are highly preferred by the tactical leaders since they specifically know the local environment, and therefore may provide an understanding of the local complexity and serve as a means for cross-cultural communication. They can give us the names of key players in the local environment, they can guide us who to trust, who not to trust, and they even can be a great source of intelligence. The interpreters also serve as the point of contact of the commander among the locals. If the commander lets them – be sure that the majority of the commanders let them for security reasons – the interpreters are the ones who arrange meetings, to whom the tactical leaders will speak to, when to speak, and most importantly, they are the guys who determine the nature of speaking in the meeting. That is, they could easily strain the tension of the meeting by creating a sort of uncompromising atmosphere, or they could make the sides relaxed and unaware of the differences in the opinions and arguments of each side. Put simply, they are the ones who moderate the meeting and determine its atmosphere. I personally witnessed many interpreters who joined chatting as the third party, who made comments and who gave advice to the parties. The incompetence of the local interpreters may, therefore, result in confusion in the COIN efforts and drastically affect their efficiency. Based on my experience, I came to conclude that in an insurgency where COIN forces do not speak the native language, a competent interpreter would be able to catch roughly 70 percent of what the tactical leader intended to say, and he would deliver roughly 40 percent of the message to the audience. During this process, let alone the intonations and body language which make the message more powerful and clearer, the message itself may get lost. More importantly, the interpreter, though he understands 90 percent of what the audience said (mainly due to his pragmatic considerations and his understanding of local politics), is inclined to filter the words of the locals, who have already filtered their words as they get in touch with the foreigners. I may assert, thus, then that the tactical leaders would be able to get only 30 percent of what the audience intended to say.

Another question regarding interpreters is that why would a local want to work as an interpreter for the COIN forces, which is a temporary and passive player in the real world of TRMEs? What would be the basic motivation for him: a mutual love and faith of COIN forces to bring stability, prosperity and democracy, or primarily pragmatist considerations?

Fully relying on my field experience, I would suggest that to be able to use the local interpreter in the intelligence business is the dream of every tactical leader. Tactical leaders imply this desire with some hesitant-looking questions to the interpreters, who in fact are waiting for this opportunity. The local interpreters, who generally not only know how to analyze the personality of their bosses, but also are fully aware of the details of the local politics, perfectly exploit this desperate need of acquiring local intelligence. If the commander is so submissive to the interpreter, imagine the power of the interpreter as the local power broker. He is 'the unofficial king' of that particular area.

Bobby Ghosh, one of the longest-serving correspondents in Iraq, states that:

> Inside Saddam's gilt and chintz-filled office, I found a Marine taking down one of Iraq's flags that hung next to the dictator's desk and asking his Kurdish interpreter to translate the green Arabic lettering that ran through the middle. I'll never know why the Kurd lied, replying 'it says Saddam Hussein' (It actually read, 'Allahu Akbar', or 'God is great'). Delighted, the Marine took the flag out to the main portico and brandished it at the crowd of Iraqis. Then he fired up a Zippo lighter and with a triumphant look announced 'this is what we will do to Saddam'.
>
> The Iraqis were aghast. None of them understood English, and all they could see was a lanky, blond American Marine about to burn their national flag. Some of them shouted at the Marine, but he mistook their anger for enthusiasm. 'Yeah! We are gonna fry his ass!' he whooped, with an exaggerated nasal Southern drawl.
>
> My interpreter and I were able – only just – to stop the Marine from setting the flag alight. When we explained what the Arabic letters really said, he turned pale. 'Oh, man, I did not know' he said, looking nervously at the crowd, which was seething with resentment. 'Can you explain that to them?' He thrust the flag into my hands and ran back indoors.[46]

This clear example would demonstrate that how the ignorance of a US soldier, which could be pardoned to some degree, since it aimed to show the decisiveness of the US Military to the local audience, could be manipulated by the ill-intentioned interpreter. More importantly, it also indicates that how a simple manipulation of an interpreter could cause strategic communication disasters for COIN forces in the field.

---

46   Bobby Gosh, 'Iraq: Missed Steps', *Time Magazine* (6 December 2010), p.42.

4

Conclusion

COIN in TRMEs may look more like a matter of tactical level rather than that of a strategic one. The details – or local ciphers left for the tactical leaders to decode how to craft local COIN strategies – of the strategic and operational plans carries utmost importance for the desired end state in a COIN campaign to be crafted for TRMEs. A COIN approach which reduces the gap between the strategic planning and the tactical facts on the ground is likely to be successful. In contrast, a COIN approach is spoiled too much with the futile strategic debates that unnecessarily complicates the visualization of a strategy since it only addresses the 'what to do' of the strategy and leaves the 'how to do' to tactical-level leaders. If SOPs specifically tailored in accordance with the *sui generis* features of TRMEs do not exist – which is generally the case – tactical leaders have only one option of turning the 'what to do' of a strategic plan into the 'how to do': that is, tactical leaders have no other alternative but to follow the footsteps of their predecessors. Following the footsteps of predecessors and strictly sticking to the 'archive' may make the tactical-level leaders feel comfortable and safer. However, the archive, or the local strategy crafted by the previous commanders on how to conduct COIN campaigns, may make the COIN forces more predictable and more prone to the manipulations of local politics. Most players in the local politics arrange their stance according to the position of COIN forces to be able to best exploit them both financially and politically.

As explained in this book, Islam, in the traditional sense, does look like a sociocultural issue rather than being a political one. There is, therefore, an immediate need to exclude it from the legacy of politics and think of it as a matter of socio-cultural study in TRMEs. When current literature on COIN is reviewed, one finds that all phenomena, specifically Islam, are excessively examined through the lenses of politics. There may be two reasons for this. The first reason which turns Islam into a politicized phenomenon in rural Afghanistan is the excessively politicized Islamic rhetoric of the *Salafi/Wahhabi* understanding, which seems to accurately address the current problems of TRMEs, but delivers vague Islamic-political promises on how to solve them. The second reason is the excessive emphasis of current COIN strategies of the CF forces in rural Afghanistan on politics. Mainly because of the traditional COIN wisdom, the CF forces seem to assess COIN as a political game between them and the insurgents. This inclination of CF solely looking at the political dimension of every phenomenon when crafting COIN strategies in rural Afghanistan seems to be the second obstacle in front of studying Islam as a matter of a socio-cultural study. Nonetheless, the monopoly of the Taliban rhetoric and the manifesto on Islam should be dissolved in rural Afghanistan. There is a high need to prove that Islam could coexist with the lifestyle proposed by the CF. This alternative lifestyle, which may be regarded as a contemporary interpretation of traditional equilibrium in the system, should be compatible with the tenets of moral codes of behavior and legitimized by the superstructure. This alternative model, endorsed with divine references, may be attractive enough to raise the curiosity of the locals in rural Afghanistan, and consequently, may help the people in TRMEs of Afghanistan unchain themselves from the arrest of the Taliban. The messages disseminated by this alternative model may beguile many in rural Afghanistan.

In the same vein, COIN in TRMEs is not a solely political-military campaign that is designed to deny insurgency. It is, instead, a blend of military and civilian efforts, which not only deals with denying insurgency but also addresses the root causes of it, a process which requires a distinctive understanding of socio-cultural, economic and psychological context. In many cases in COIN, the civilian efforts constitute the avenues of approach to the desired end state, while military efforts play the enabler role in the construction of these avenues. The complexity of COIN efforts in TRMEs, by and large, highly calls for an interdisciplinary approach, in which a broad knowledge of a wide variety of related disciplines are synthesized appropriately. That is, an accurate and clear assessment of insurgency requires a deep and shared understanding of cultural, ideological, religious, demographic, geographic, sociological and psychological dynamics that effect insurgency.

Certainly all insurgencies do have an important political component, but that should be considered only as one part of the picture. Insurgency also fulfills the socio-cultural, economic and psychological needs, which is a perfect case in TRMEs. It provides, for instance, a source of income out of proportion to what the insurgents could otherwise earn, particularly for the lower ranks – and it provides a source of identity and empowerment for those with few other sources of these things. Without a gun, most insurgent foot soldiers are simply poor, uneducated, disempowered, and disengaged youths with no prospects. Insurgency changes that. It makes insurgents important, powerful and a defender of a high cause, which aims to purify the exogenous inputs that spoiled the society with divine references – and it provides them with a livelihood and a sense of belongingness. On the other hand, insurgency may also be aptly exploited by the players of local politics and may turn into a good means to make a fortune or to consolidate power for local power brokers. Local politics may drive the insurgency and COIN efforts, and the COIN forces may turn out to be the pioneers in the local political chess game. There may be good allies who side with COIN forces against insurgency, but these allies may seek for turning their alliance with COIN forces into financial or political bonuses, or to take advantage of it to intimidate the local populace. Regarding any insurgency in TRMEs as solely a political military two-party campaign between the insurgents and COIN forces, and trying to address it at the strategic or operational level, may lead to false conclusions on the nature of the insurgency. Therefore, an analysis of the present conflict in TRMEs cannot be limited to the insurgency and insurgents; indeed, the insurgency should be understood as merely a symptom of deep-rooted political and socio-cultural divisions, as well as pernicious economic interests in TRMEs – hence countering the insurgency is not fighting the insurgency *per se*, but understanding these multiple types of strife and responding in kind. That is why there is a high need to study social roles, group status, institutions and relations among different population groups, often in non-elite and non-state-based frameworks. The first step of this study may be an accurate, unbiased and comprehensive analysis of the superstructure, and moral codes of behavior that shape in TRMEs. All values and norms in the superstructure, firstly, may be categorized into threefold: the ones that are rooted from Islam, the ones that are rooted from the traditional tribal codes and the ones that would be rooted from both. After classifying all norms and values, the social roles of each player in the TRMEs may be examined meticulously. The ones, for instance, such as traditional tribal leaders, or the *Khan* class; the village leaders as the intra-tribe and community leaders; and elders, or the gray beards in the advisory position, constitute the executive branch. The traditional Islamic networks such as the *Sufi* ones traditionally function as a legislative forum and help create new norms and values compatible with the superstructure – and the *mullah* class, which traditionally functions as the judiciary branch that solves every socio-political and economic dispute (with the consent of the executive branch in most cases) – is the third tier in the system. The delicate balance of the superstructure could only be achieved by first, the peaceful co-existence of those legitimate players, and second, their directing of efforts for the common good of the people they lead. After studying the social roles of each player in the system, which may, more or less, vary from one TRME to another one, the phase of analyzing the relations of every player to one another would be implemented. A comprehensive analysis of the relations of every player in the system and the institutions that constitute the type and extent of relations would endow accurate insights for achieving the objective of acquiring a framework to better understand how the local governance is carried out in that particular TRME.

Since traditional COIN wisdom views insurgency as a political rivalry between the host nation government and the insurgents, current COIN strategy of the CF in rural Afghanistan stresses the need for a state-centric political reform in TRMEs of Afghanistan. This is a necessary objective as a desired long-term end state but irrelevant at the moment since there is no, or there is a trivial passive role, of the central government in the local governance in many TRMEs of Afghanistan. In *FM 3-24*, 'the end state' is a 'secure and stable environment' in any COIN campaign. One should notice, then, that the end state should be divorced from any political or ideological suggestion, which points that there is no superiority of one particular political system over another. Stated another way, a stable and secure environment may not necessarily mean a state-centric democratic end state in TRMEs. A comprehensive COIN strategy precisely tailored for any particular TRME should take into account this simple fact. The attempts to impose the central government as an important player in the local governance would create frustration and alienation in the society since there is no room for the central government in the governance in the traditional sense, at least for now. One should notice as well that all solutions are local in TRMEs; that is why strategists should tailor a COIN strategy for the people where they live and consider the local dynamics. That is why any one-size fits all COIN strategy crafted in Kabul only addresses strategic and operational considerations and may be futile.

Firstly, it is time for the international community to come to the realization that there is only one solution for peace in rural Afghanistan, and it's an Afghan solution. That is, Afghans in TRMEs should be the ones who play the leading roles in the strategy and all efforts of COIN forces should be kept as low-profile and low-visibility in this 'made in Afghanistan' solution. This strategy should also be tailored as a community-based approach. Geographic proximity: the people living in the same village or district should be the focal point in this approach. Engaging only selected tribes or individuals may alienate other tribal structures and other key figures in TRMEs, and therefore drastically change the local balance of power in the system. To build a strategy relying on one particular tribe or individual and their sustained support by COIN forces may result in the emergence of warlords in the system.

A comprehensive strategy should make the rhetoric of the *Wahhabi/Salafi* understanding irrelevant not in material and purely military terms but also in socio-political, religious, socio-psychological and economic areas. A strategy should also regulate equilibrium in the superstructure by turning religious leaders to their traditional spiritual guidance roles in legislative and judicial areas and recreating the responsive *Khan* class at the seat of the execution.

When history, socio-political and economic background, geographic and demographic features of Afghanistan are taken into account, a COIN strategy which relies on a government-imposed top-down approach is highly likely to falter. A strategy for TRMEs in rural Afghanistan should be tailored with a bottom-up approach, by means of which the CF may turn out to be an active player in the real world. Whereas a top-down strategy includes outside actors allocating resources to the highest political and military level in that particular state, a bottom-up approach allocates resources to promote local leaders and assist them in providing security and services to the local population. The socio-political reform route should be pursued bottom-up. The bottom-up approach aims to connect local political entities to the central government, when the environment is matured. Put it differently, while a top-down strategy aims to spread influence of the government institutions to the periphery, a bottom-up approach allocates resources to promote the influence of the political institutions in the periphery to the expense of center. This said, the current approach of fixing Afghanistan as a whole and through strengthening the institutions of the central government to stand on their own would be more likely a task that will require a decades-long commitment.

There may be a legitimate concern that too much focus at the local level may result in the collapse of the central government in Kabul and destabilize Afghanistan. The strategy proposed in this book would, therefore, be regarded as a futile one, which is at odds with the policy of creating a strong central government. Nonetheless, one should accept that change acceptable by the TRMEs of Afghanistan will simply not come from the central government, which has still been described as an 'alien' political entity that promotes corruption by the rural population.

As the soldiers of modern militaries, we are conditioned to ask questions such as: what should the army be prepared for and how should it be armed? We have no doubt about the aim of an operation – the destruction of the enemy. Afghanistan, however, shows that we need a new kind of thinking and new cognitive templates on the use of military power in COIN operations. As emphasized in this book, the operational level, playing a bridge role in the traditional sense, connecting the tactical level to the strategic-political one is melting. That is why, the gap between the strategic-political level and the tactical level is widening, a trend the first consequence of which is the inability to translate tactical achievements on the ground into sustainable political end states in COIN settings. This book thus suggests that, to overcome this setback, we should seek for new cognitive templates and concepts in military studies critically engaging problems at hand, and to some extent, to problematize those with military designing. Military designing to set the stage and to define the operational theater should be the very first step of military efforts in any COIN setting.

Indeed, Afghanistan has underlined the distinction between 'planning' and 'design'. While both activities seek to formulate ways to bring about preferable futures, they are cognitively different. Planning applies established procedures to solve a largely understood problem within an accepted framework. Design, on the other hand, enquires into the nature of a problem in order to conceive a framework for solving that problem. In general, planning is problem-solving, while designing is problem-setting. Where planning focuses on generating a plan – a series of executable actions – design focuses on learning about the nature of an unfamiliar problem. At the initial phase, one may suggest that CF were too busy to solve problems in Afghanistan with the traditional cognitive and material tools to such an extent that they could not find time to define the nature of the conflict in Afghanistan and set the problems in the Afghani way. Afghanistan proved that in hybrid settings, general planning is not enough to adapt to a new situation. In Afghanistan, one needs new designs, preferably asymmetric ones, which zoom closer into the nature of an unfamiliar conflict in order to conceive a framework for problem-solving. Unfortunately, modern militaries still fall short of learning the nature and characteristics of new and unconventional problems as they traditionally and blindly aim to prepare for the present conflict as if it were the previous war.

That is why, this book, presenting a *critique,* or a problematization of 'our way of COIN in Afghanistan', is a problem-setting one rather than a problem-solving one. The Islamic State's (IS) attempts to jump in Afghanistan clearly shows that COIN in hybrid settings like Afghanistan will be morphing beyond our current conceptions.

The evolving character of COIN operations thus will present an intellectual challenge ahead of us. Unfortunately, the soldiers in COIN settings should find their way by themselves without clear political directives on how to use military power in getting increasingly complex COIN settings. It is the 'military designing capability', the remedy offered by this book, that modern militaries of the world should debate more on to increase their situational awareness in future COIN settings.

Modern Western militaries are conditioned to ask questions like: what should the army be prepared for? How should it be armed? How can effective military planning be applied to achieve the political objectives? This book, however, suggests that, in future COIN settings, these are not relevant questions anymore. The most favorite ones are: how can we set the problems to define the security environment at hand? Which sort of military design can we 'tailor' for this particular security environment? Why, how and through which mechanisms can we adapt to this time and context-specific design? Simply, it is the design we should adapt to, and we should not make the design adapt to 'our ways of thinking and doing things'. That is why, nowadays, what the modern Western militaries need more of are 'military designers' – not 'military planners'.

Bibliography

Arnold, Anthony, *Afghanistan's Two-Party Communism: Parcham and Khalq* (Stanford: Hoover Press, 1983).
Astarjian, Henry D., *The Struggle for Kirkuk* (Westport: Praeger Security International, 2007).
Baram, Amatzia, 'The Iraqi Tribes and the Post-Saddam System', *Saban Center for Middle East Policy at the Brookings Institution* (8 July 2003).
Barfield, Thomas, 'Is Afghanistan 'Medieval'?', *Foreign Policy* (2 June 2010).
Belasco, Amy, 'The Cost of Iraq, Afghanistan, and Other Global War on Terror Operations Since 9/11', *CFR Report* (8 December 2014).
Brachman, Jarret, 'Watching Watchers', *Foreign Policy* (February 2010).
Bruno, Greg, 'A Tribal Strategy in Afghanistan', *Council on Foreign Relations Publication* (7 November 2008).
Crile, George, *Charlie Wilson's War: The Extraordinary Story of How the Wildest Man in Congress and a Rogue CIA Agent Changed the History of Our Times* (New York: Grove Press, 2003).
Cooley, John K., *Unholy Wars: Afghanistan, America and International Terrorism* (London: Pluto Press, 2002).
Dupree, Louis, *Afghanistan* (Oxford University Press, 2002).
Dorronsoro, Gilles, *Revolution Unending: Afghanistan, 1979 to Present* (Columbia University Press, 2005).
Edwards, David B., *Before Taliban: Genealogies of the Afghan Jihad* (Los Angeles: University of California Press, 2002).
Enloe, Cynthia H., and Mostafa Rejai, 'Nation-states and State-Nations', *International Studies Quarterly*, Vol. 13, No. 2 (June 1969).
Ernst, Carl W., *Following Muhammad: Rethinking Islam in the Contemporary World* (London: University of North Carolina Press, 2003).
Ewans, Sir Martin, *Afghanistan: A New History* (London: Routledge Curzon, 2002).
Freeman, Christopher, 'Introduction: Security, Governance and State Building in Afghanistan', *International Peacekeeping*, Vol. 14, No. 1 (January 2007).
Galula, David, *Counterinsurgency Warfare: Theory and Practice* (Westport, Connecticut: Praeger Security International, 2006).

Gant, Jim, *A Strategy for Success in Afghanistan: One tribe at a time* (Nine Sisters Imports: Los Angeles, 2009).
Giustozzi, Antonio, *Empires of Mud: Wars and Warlords in Afghanistan* (New York: Oxford University Press, 2009).
Griffin, Michael, *Reaping the Whirlwind: The Taliban Movement in Afghanistan* (London: Pluto Press, 2001).
Gohari, M. J., *The Taliban: Ascent to Power* (Oxford: Oxford University Press, 2001).
Goodson, Larry P., *Afghanistan's Endless War: State Failure, Regional Politics and the Rise of the Taliban* (Seattle: University of Washington Press, 2001).
Gurcan, Metin, 'Between Heaven and Earth: Field Observations Relating to Counterinsurgency in Tribalized Rural Muslim Environments', *Dynamics of Asymmetric Conflict*, 2:2 (2011).
Gurcan, Metin, 'Seeing the Other Side of the COIN: Problematization of 'Our' COIN Efforts in Afghanistan', *Istanbul Policy Center (IPC) Report* (February 2016).
Hammes, Thomas X., *The Sling and the Stone: On War in the 21st Century* (St. Paul, MN: Zenith Press, 2004).
Heper, Metin, *State and Kurds in Turkey* (New York: Palgrave Macmillan, 2008).
Holt, Frank L., *Into the Land of Bones: Alexander the Great in Afghanistan* (Los Angeles: University of California Press, 2006).
Hunter, Shireen, 'Religion, Politics and Security in CA', *SAIS Review* (Summer 2001).
Jawad, Nassim, *Afghanistan: A Nation of Minorities* (London, UK: Minority Rights Group International. Manchester Free Press, February 1992).
Johnson, Rob, *Oil, Islam and Conflict* (London: Reaktion Books, 2007).
Kalyvas, Stathis N., *The Logic of Violence in Civil War* (Cambridge: Cambridge University Press, 2006).
Kilcullen, David, *The Accidental Guerilla: Fighting Small Wars in the Midst of a Big One* (London: Hurst, 2009).
Kilcullen, David, 'Twenty-Eight articles: Fundamentals of Company-Level Counterinsurgency', *Military Review* (May-June 2006).
McDowall, David, *A Modern History of the Kurds* (New York: St. Martin's Press, 1996).
Nagl, John A., *Learning to Eat Soup with a Knife: Counterinsurgency Lessons from Malaya and Vietnam* (Chicago: University of Chicago Press, 2005).
O'Hanlon, Michael, 'Staying Power: The U.S. Mission in Afghanistan beyond 2011', *Foreign Affairs* (October-December 2010).
Ozcan, Ali Nihat, 'PKK Party Congress Sets Long-Term Strategy Based on Threat Perceptions', *Terrorism Monitor*, Vol. 6, No. 2 (2008).
Poliakov, Sergei P., *Everyday Islam: Religion and Tradition in Rural Central Asia* (New York: M. E. Sharp, 1992).
Qutb, Sayyid, *Milestones* (Kazi Publications, 2003).
Rafiq, Arif, 'A Muslim Solution for Afghanistan', *Christian Science Monitor* (6 October 2009).

Rand Report, 'Ungoverned Territories', *Rand Corporation* (2007).
Rashid, Ahmed, 'Back to Feudalism', *Far Eastern Economic Review* (13 July 1989).
——, *Taliban: Militant Islam, Oil, and Fundamentalism in Central Asia* (London: Yale University Press, 2001).
——, *Jihad: the Rise of Militant Islam in Central Asia* (New York: Penguin Books, 2002).
——, *Descent into Chaos* (London: Penguin Books, 2008).
Rubin, Barnett R., *The Fragmentation of Afghanistan* (London: Yale University Press, 2002).
Tripp, Charles, *A History of Iraq* (New York: Cambridge University Press, 2007).
Zaeef, Abdul Salam, *My life With the Taliban* (Melbourne: Scribe Publications, 2010).

Military Manuals

'US Counterinsurgency', *Field Manual 3-24* (2006).
'US Government Counterinsurgency Guide', *US Government Interagency Counterinsurgency Initiative* (January 2009).
'Counterinsurgency Guide', *US State Department* (January 2009).

Index

Afghan National Security Forces xvi, 81, 93
Afghanistan i-iii, vii-xvi, xviii-xxvii, 30-34, 36-38, 40-43, 45, 48-52, 61-62, 65-92, 94-96, 99-102, 104-124, 126-130, 132-134
Ahmadzai, Muhammad Najibullah 37-38, 81
akhlaq xxvi, 39, 58, 66, 75, 77, 85-86
Alexander the Great 67, 133
al-Qaeda ix, xix-xx, 45, 47, 81, 94-95, 100, 114, 119-120
Anatolia xiii, 38, 41
Arabian Peninsula 46, 48

Baghdad 51, 54, 116
Bagram Air Base 82, 118
Barzan 41, 57
Biden, Joe xix, 94
bin Laden, Osama 47-48, 81
Bosnia 40, 79
burqa 32-33, 77

Central Asia xiv, 37, 40-42, 48, 69, 71, 79, 84-85, 124, 133-134
China 40, 69
Christianity 34, 48
CIA viii, xiv, 69, 71, 78, 80, 132
Clausewitzian xix, 94
Coalition Forces (CF) ix-x, xii-xiii, xv-xvi, xviii, xix, xxiv-xxvii, 51, 67, 70, 73, 82, 86, 88, 90, 95, 100-102, 105-106, 108-110, 112-123, 126-130
Combined Forces Command-Afghanistan (CFA-A) 82, 107

Communism 77-80, 83, 132
Congressional Research Service (CRS) 46-48, 108
Counterinsurgency (COIN) i, vii, xi-xiii, xv-xxvii, 49, 62, 68, 71-72, 92-100, 102, 104-116, 118-119, 122-131, 133
Counterinsurgency i-iii, ix-xi, 89, 94, 96-97, 99, 114, 132-134

Department of Defense (DoD) 108, 117
Durrani 71, 84

Feudalism 34, 38, 134
Forward Operation 74, 117

Gant, Major Jim xii, xxi, 121
Germany 108, 115
Ghilzai 41, 71, 77

hadith 41-42, 44, 62
Hanafi School 42, 71, 79
Hazaras 65, 71
Hussein, Saddam 51, 62, 125, 132

Improvised Explosive Device (IED) 56, 112-113
International Security Assistance Force (ISAF) i, 82, 97, 107-108
Iran 41, 47-48, 69
Iraq i-ii, xii-xiii, xx, xxvi, 34, 37-38, 40-43, 45, 51, 53-54, 56-57, 59, 61-63, 104, 111, 116, 118-120, 122, 124-125, 132, 134
Iraqi Security Forces 51, 63

Islam x, xiv, xx-xxi, xxiv, xxvi-xxvii,
   35-43, 45-50, 57-58, 66-67, 71, 77-79,
   83-86, 88, 90, 102, 126-128, 132-134

Jamaat-I Islami 46, 77
Japan 39, 108
Jihad xiv, xx, 43, 53, 77-79, 81, 83, 87,
   112, 132, 134

Kabul ix, 38, 67-68, 71, 74, 77, 81-83,
   89-90, 107, 118, 129-130
Kandahar 71, 87, 118
Kazakhstan i-ii, xiii, xxvi, 110
Khalq 76-77, 132
Khan, Mohammad Sardar Daoud 37,
   76-77
King Zahir Shah 76, 78
Kurdish Workers Party (PKK) 51-52,
   133
Kyrgyzstan i-ii, xiii, xxvi

Marxist 51, 76
Mecca 41, 48-49
Medina 48-49
Mediterranean 41, 118
Middle East xiv, 79, 132
Mujahideen 79-81, 83-84, 88
Mullah 44-45, 50, 83-84, 86, 128
Muslim Brotherhood 46, 77

namus 32-33, 40
North Atlantic Treaty Organization
   (NATO) ix, 82, 97, 107-108, 114,
   123

Obama, President Barack viii, xii, xix, 74,
   95, 114
Omar, *Mullah* Muhammad 83-84

Pakistan ix, xix, 45-46, 48, 52, 69-72,
   77-78, 81, 83-84, 87, 94
Parcham 76-77, 132
Pashtun 40, 77, 119
Petraeus, General David 97, 120

Prophet Muhammad xxiv, 35, 41, 43, 45,
   48-49, 59, 84

Qandahar 84, 88
Quran 41, 43-45, 49, 58-59, 79-80, 84,
   106

Reagan, President Ronald 78-79
Rumi, Mawlana xv, 67, 74-75

Salafi xiii, 45-47, 65-66, 78, 102, 126,
   129
Saudi Arabia 45-49, 83
Sharia Law 32-33, 40-42, 44-45, 59, 61,
   79, 86, 106
Sheikh Ali 59-60
Shia xviii, 41-45, 48, 65, 71
Shia School 42-43, 45
Soviet Invasion 31, 48, 71, 78, 80-82, 84,
   88, 90, 123
Soviet Union 76-78, 81
Standardized Operational Procedures
   (SOPs) xvii-xviii, 126
Sufi 43-45, 48, 50, 67, 74, 76, 84, 128
Sunni xviii, 41-42, 45, 48, 71, 120

Talib, Ali ibn Abi xxiv, 42-43, 51, 58-60,
   133
Taliban viii-x, xii, xv-xvi, xix, xxii, xxiv-
   xxvi, 32-33, 50-51, 68, 71, 73-75, 78-79,
   81-91, 94, 100, 102, 106, 110, 112,
   116-122, 127, 132-134
tore xxvi, 39
Tribalized Rural Muslim Environment
   (TRME) i, vii, ix-x, xiii-xvi, xvii, xx,
   xviii-xxiv, xxvi-xxvii, 29, 30-35, 37-41,
   43-45, 47-50, 53-66, 76, 78, 80, 83, 85,
   88-90, 93, 98-99, 103-107, 110, 114,
   116, 118, 121-124, 126-130
Turkey i, xxvi, 37-38, 40, 43, 51-52, 133
Turkish Special Forces i-ii, xiii, 110

United Nations (UN) 37, 48, 63, 77-78,
   81-82, 107-108

United States (US) 48, 76-78, 82, 108, 115, 119
urf ad'at xxvi, 39
US Forces ix, 62
US Special Forces xii, xix, xxi, 79, 94, 121
Uzbekistan 69-70

Wahhabism 45-49, 65-66, 78, 83, 102, 126, 129
warlordism xxii, 33, 91, 121-122
Washington 48, 68, 70-71, 107, 115, 121, 133

Zaeef, Abdul Salam 87, 134